HIGH TEA
ON THE
CUNARD
QUEENS

HIGH TEA
ON THE
CUNARD
QUEENS

*A Light-Hearted Look
at Life at Sea*

PAUL CURTIS

The
History
Press

Front cover: Cunard 'Getting there is half the fun' poster/© Alamy/Shawshots

Back cover: Cunard '1930s' and *'Berengaria'* postcards/© Cunard

First published 2019

The History Press
97 St George's Place, Cheltenham,
Gloucestershire, GL50 3QB
www.thehistorypress.co.uk

British Library Cataloguing in Publication Data.
A catalogue record for this book is available from the British Library.

ISBN 978 0 7509 9055 4

Typesetting and origination by The History Press
Printed in Europe

Ships that pass in the night,
and speak each other in passing,
only a signal shown,
and a distant voice in the darkness;
So on the ocean of life,
we pass and speak one another,
only a look and a voice,
then darkness again and a silence.

HENRY WADSWORTH LONGFELLOW

CONTENTS

THE CUNARD QUEENS

This spread: Top left to bottom right: Berengaria, *1912–1938 (named after a British Queen)*; Queen Mary, *1936–1967 (Paul Curtis)*; Queen Elizabeth, *1940–1968 (Paul Curtis)*; Queen Elizabeth 2, *1969–2008. (Murgatroyd49, CC.SA 4.0 via WikimediaCommons)*; Queen Mary 2, *2004. (Paul Curtis)*; Queen Victoria (© *E. Levavasseur /Adobe Stock*); Queen Elizabeth *(Natallia Yaumenenka, © eAlisa /Adobe Stock); The New Queen, 2022 (Cunard)*.

YE OLDE ORIGINAL QUEEN MARY

Mary Mary, quite contrary
How does your garden grow
With silver bells and cockleshells
And pretty maids all in a row.

In playgrounds across England and around the world, young schoolchildren have innocently recited this nursery rhyme for generations. While not wishing to spoil harmless enjoyment, let's note that it is claimed the Mary alluded to here is Mary Tudor – or none other than (roll of drums) 'Bloody Mary'.

The daughter of King Henry VIII, Mary, unlike her dad, was a staunch Catholic. It is thought the poem was a heavily veiled protest by her Protestant subjects; disguised, as even the slightest hint of criticism could get your head chopped off.

In this interpretation, the garden alludes to the increasing size of graveyards to accommodate those who dared to adhere to the Protestant faith. The 'silver bells' and 'cockleshells' were colloquialisms for instruments of torture. The silver bells were thumbscrews, the cockleshells were instruments attached to the male genitals.

The 'maids' were the original guillotines – a technological breakthrough of the day for beheading. It was also called the maiden as, by getting rid of the menfolk, it created quite a few. Until the maiden, beheading a victim could be a tad troublesome. The victim, often not enamoured with the deal, might have to be chased by the axeman around the scaffold. It could take up to eleven blows to completely sever the head. Much better with one swift, clean chop. See what technology can do for you?

Maybe it would have been better for all if Mary had stuck with her little lamb.

FOREWORD

There have been many books written about the Cunard Line over the years: very well-written accounts documenting the company's long and illustrious history, retracing the iconic red-funnelled liners that have criss-crossed the world's oceans for the past 178 years.

High Tea on the Cunard Queens is not just another elegantly bound maritime history book, nor a nice ornament for the coffee table; it's written with a meaningful intent. This is a first-hand version of how things were in the golden age of ocean travel on the Queens, a bygone era that can be relived in this book by those who missed it the first time around. From turning the first page you will have 'boarded' a Cunard Queen. You'll hear the ship's foghorn booming, the commotion on the crew decks below, the champagne corks popping, and the afternoon's white-gloved tea-pouring. The author, a former Ship's Entertainment Officer and now seasoned passenger, will give you the unedited insider's story of working and travelling on the greatest liners that have graced the North Atlantic and their modern, very different, successors today.

It tells the story of the shaky start in life for both *Queen Mary* and *Queen Elizabeth*, their service to King and Country, their rise post-war to reign over the North Atlantic and their demise with the onset of the jet age. The story continues with the birth of the legendary *QE2*, the trials and tribulations that accompanied her birth to the current Queens that proudly reign on the high seas and one of which I have the privilege of commanding. *High Tea on the Cunard Queens* will appeal to both seasoned passengers and to those who have never even stepped on board a ship (yet) as well as to members of the crew past and present, as they know what's written is 'spot on'.

I congratulate Paul Curtis on *High Tea on the Cunard Queens*, which is written with an unapologetic but essential sense of humour, topped off with lots of nautical anecdotes that you perhaps always wondered about but will now get to finally uncover.

Now all that remains for you to do is to sit back, relax and enjoy the voyage ahead – bon voyage!

Captain Aseem A. Hashmi MNM
Master, *Queen Elizabeth*

Captain Aseem Hashmi. (Cunard)

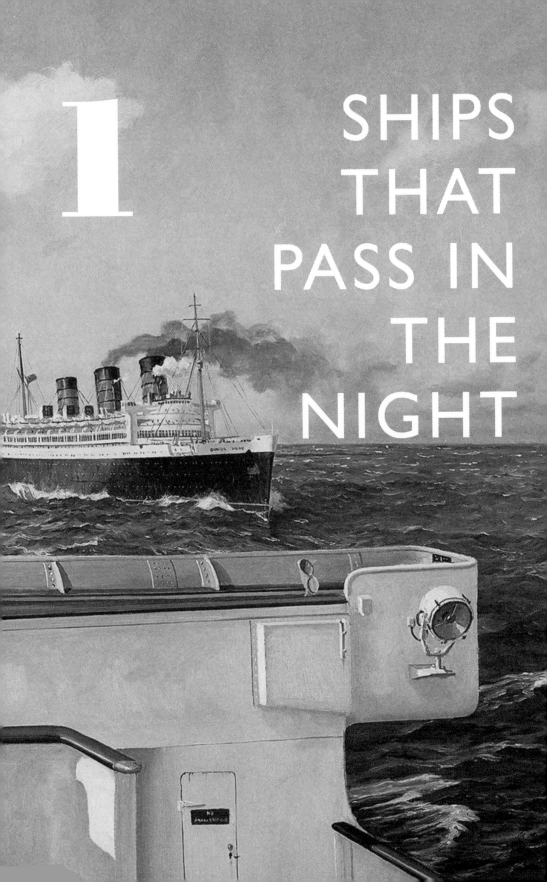

1

SHIPS THAT PASS IN THE NIGHT

GRACIOUS, IT WAS A LONG TIME AGO. I am a young man, dressed in my work clothes – dinner jacket and black tie – leaning my weight against the heavy door opening onto the boat deck. It is the wee small hours of the morning on 25 September 1967. Blasts of rain hit my face, but I see the white-capped waves continually rising and falling into darkness. It is what my father used to call weather cold enough to make brass monkeys testicularly challenged. We are in the middle of the North Atlantic and I'm out here in the cold, when I should be snug in bed. But this is a major milestone in passenger shipping history and I don't want to miss it.

I am on the world's greatest and largest liner: *Queen Mary*. Soon we will cross paths with the other ship that claims to be the world's greatest and largest liner: *Queen Elizabeth*. *Mary's* crafty crew quibble over the measurements used and seek to bend statistics to their advantage. Okay, *Elizabeth* is a teensy bit bigger. I will get over it.

Since 1946, on their respective voyages between England and the United States, these sisters have crossed midway nearly a thousand times. This was not always within sight, but as this is a very special but sad occasion, tonight they most definitely will be. The unthinkable has happened: both ships are now on the auctioneer's block and tonight's crossing will be for the last time.

There are only a few people on deck: three or four small groups, seeking ineffective shelter under the lifeboats, huddling along the rail, gazing steadfastly out to sea like a row of phlegmatic penguins. The number of passengers is at half strength and most of them are just unaware, or not particularly interested in the significance of this moment.

Of course, our thousand crew all know. It has been topping the ship's rumour charts for months. But at this hour, many are on duty, while others are just too sad and disillusioned to be out here and bear witness to the end of their lives at sea. After all, it's the middle of the night and all we will do is catch a mere glimpse of the other ship's lights, swishing past at a combined speed of 60mph.

Fortunately, our wait is short. Both ships are on schedule. As we cross, each momentarily flashes her deck lights. At 1,000ft apart, it is more eerie than spectacular. On our bridge, Captain John Treasure-Jones doffs his cap to Commodore Geoffrey Marr on the bridge of *Queen Elizabeth*. The salute is returned, but in the darkness goes unseen. The ships sound rumbling baritone blasts on their whistles saying goodbye. Tonight, that deep throaty roar, which can be felt on board and carries for 10 miles, sounds muted and forlorn.

Within minutes, she is gone. Just like the movies, *Elizabeth*'s lights fade to black. The End. Roll the credits: no more grand liners, no more ships this big, no more magic and romance in crossing from the Old World to the New. Death by airlines.

Instead of four formal evening dinners, followed by dancing and entertainment, travellers will forever more be crammed and cocooned into narrow aluminium tubes to be hurled through the sky like javelins.

Sadly, we straggle below for glasses of consolation at the bar. We mutter regrets at the end or our way of life and proclaim that the glory days of passenger shipping have just hit the dustbin of history. Or so we thought.

There was great pride in being a member of a Queen's company. These were no idle cruise ships aimlessly trolling around a few islands. They were magnificent liners, strong ships with a purpose, a schedule to keep in all weathers, and we had a job to do, to get people safely across the vast North Atlantic dividing the Old World from the New.

The whole world held both Queens in so much awe and respect that working on them was the holy grail of going to sea. They were the biggest and fastest. They were steeped in history, played vital roles easing Britain's Great Depression and served their county with honour during the Second World War.

In peacetime, everyone from royalty, world leaders, the rich and the famous to the migrants and the poor took passage on their life-changing journeys. For more than three decades the two ships reliably criss-crossed the North Atlantic in all weathers and with religious punctuality. No other shipping line could match us.

But for the last few months, an ominous dark cloud had dampened the crew's normal cheer. We saw our passenger numbers rapidly declining. With a groan, we had to concede that on some crossings we had more crew than passengers. There might have been more time for crew partying, but stewards saw their tips vaporising into thin air.

From 1954 to 1965, the number of people taking airline passage from Europe to the USA rose from 600,000 to 4 million. In the same period, the number of passengers on the two Queens dropped from 1 million to 650,000. Our guest list was falling faster than the Mexican peso.

LOOKING FOR A BIT OF COMMON

To fight back, Cunard tried to modernise itself. My own job, for instance, was as an entertainments officer. Previously, this duty had been done by uniformed pursers, sourced from the best homes and schools and thus able to seamlessly blend in with the lords, ladies and high society on the passenger list. I, on the other hand, had only ever seen pictures of such people in the doctor's waiting-room copies of *Tatler* magazine. But that same high society was the first to desert us and convert to the novelty of flying.

Seeking new markets, Cunard began to pitch to younger and more ordinary folk. With this in mind, I am sure that my interviewing panel was looking for a new entertainments officer: someone a bit common; someone not from their customary elitist gene pool. They wanted an ordinary bloke, someone who had been to neither Oxford nor Cambridge, someone the unwashed hoi polloi could relate to. They hired me.

I thought the offer to join was great. My seaman's book already showed five years on passenger ships, but these had been either Greek, Italian, Norwegian, Swedish or Dutch. *Queen Mary* was my first British ship. At last, the coveted Blue Ensign. Rule Britannia and all that. And what a ship! The crème de la crème of the North Atlantic liners. Only 23 and I had arrived. Hallelujah!

RUMOURS, RUMOURS

But no sooner had I signed on than my joy was scuppered by whispers about my new ship's future. Aboard ship, wild crew rumours are the daily bread, and heavily buttering that bread was a pastime at which the British crew of *Queen Mary* excelled. The more absurd and shocking, the better. The rumours flew faster than Usain Bolt closing an endorsement deal. Twitter looks snail-paced.

Fake news? Of course, at sea with no radio, television or newspapers, we had to make our own. But the real trouble with the constant rumours was that some of them proved true. Damn.

Where do ship rumours start? In my time, it could never be tracked down as some clever chappies can do today with that internet gizmo.

The Mary's *telephone switchboard.*

Although we had no internet, we did have ship's telephone switchboard operators. They knew everything.

In these days before direct dialling, phone connections were made by young ladies armed with combination microphone headsets and flying arms that moved in a blur, quickly stretching out and plucking multiple leads one after another from socket to socket in a tangled zigzag maze of confusion. Overhearing everything, these multitasking-enabled girls were armed with dangerous knowledge.

One of my former friends at sea was a tall, Amazon-built Dutch switchboard girl with an amazing ability to perfectly mimic not only male and female voices, but to do so in dozens of accents. Bad enough, you might think, but she could do it in three different languages as well. With a few drinks inside her, she was great fun at a party. With or without a drink, she was also armed with a quick and wicked sense of humour. You crossed her at your peril.

The smallest slight might result, during the wee small hours of the morning, in her poor victim answering a call from the captain ordering them to report immediately to the bridge. Hurriedly getting dressed with fear and trepidation, the long journey to the bridge would end in finding a confused and cranky captain wondering what the hell was going on.

Whatever the source, the stories ran from the moment you got up to the time you went back to bed. At first, I couldn't believe the rumours that the Queens were to be sold. The mere idea was ridiculous. They were the pride of Britain. By gad sir, what utter nonsense. Pah.

But as the voyages passed by, the stories intensified. What was to happen to us? This was our home, our way of life. Do we go to another ship? But that would mean demotion as there weren't any other 80,000-ton liners. And even if we did manage to get a job on one of those piddling little cruise ships, it wouldn't last long either as they were also getting the chop.

Most likely, if we wanted to stay with a life at sea, we would end up on some rusty old freighter, or even a smelly and highly explosive tanker. As an entertainments officer, few prospects for me there. I would be down in the crew's quarters, calling bingo for eight hairy stokers who, between them, had not a single word of English. Still, better than wearing a red coat in a landlocked Butlin's holiday camp.

There were six of us in my department: cruise director, social directress, assistant cruise director, assistant social directress and then one entertainments officer for tourist class and another, me, for cabin class.

Cabin class was akin to the business section on today's airlines: a sort of no man's land for the vaguely educated with an expense account. They sit between the no-expense-account backpackers in tourist and the toffs in first who don't need an expense account.

So, my role of calling bingo and novelty dancing for the middle classes was going down the gurgler. However, my cruise director was reassuring. He patted me on the head, 'Don't you fret yourself young man, you will be transferred to the *Elizabeth*. We still have a need for people like you.' See, they were still pitching for the common touch.

But, in May 1967, both Queens' captains were handed special sealed orders to be opened only after the ships sailed from port. Why? Well, the company wanted to make sure the crews did in fact sail. For the official announcement was the sentence of doom: both ships were to be sold.

Again, I was told to hang on. A new Cunarder was under construction, albeit a bit smaller. She was the *QE2*, but the remorseless rumour mills ground on. It seemed that while still on the building blocks, she was to be put up for sale and that she would never sail under the Cunard flag. Given everything else that went before, you had to believe it.

This was totally disheartening. There was an enormous sense of crew patriotism aboard liners of all nationalities and rivalry was intense. It was a measure of a country's prestige to build the biggest, fastest and most luxurious ships. The investments were so costly that governments would assist their national shipping companies to make sure their country was as good as or better than any other.

All the nationality crews were proud of their ships. There is a very special relationship between crew members and their ship. It is their home. More than that, it is their mother as well. Sailors can go ashore, have a wild binge and spend every last penny they had. In land jobs you would then be destitute. But for us, the mother ship would take us in, provide a bed, put food on the table and see that we had proper clothes and washed behind our ears until the next payday. Rich again, we would go ashore in the next port keen and eager to repeat the whole process. On these forays, we would often meet crews from other ships and over a drink compare notes. But on the Queens, we always felt superior. Our ships were the biggest and best. We were top dogs, walking taller than the rest. But now it was us that faced the axe.

THE END IS NIGH

Of course, other European liners were facing trouble too and their crews were (if you will forgive the expression) in the same boat. On one of my past ships, I became friends with a wine sommelier. Remember them? They used to patrol the restaurant in a red waistcoat with a silver wine-tasting cup hanging from their neck on a heavy gold chain. They usually also had oversized and blistering red noses.

Part of my friend's duties included looking after a huge tureen of Dorset Blue Vinney cheese displayed at the entrance to the first-class dining room. Expensive stuff.

He was from Sweden and as I came from a town closely bordering Dorset, he thought that gave me all the necessary qualifications to best advise him on the selection of the red wine needed to keep the prized Stilton at just the right crumbly texture. I had not done Stilton Keeping 101 and I really didn't have a clue. However, as access to copious quantities of good free wine was involved, I hastily agreed. I'm good natured like that.

After dinner and when the dining room had emptied, he would join me at my table with the cheese and a few bottles. We would carefully examine the Stilton for texture and taste and then ritualistically sample a few of the finest wines to determine the best for the task in hand.

With increasingly merry quips, we would create our own blends of Shiraz, Cabernet Sauvignon and Merlot. Sometimes, not quite sure we had it exactly right, we would find it necessary to check the wine list and open another couple of bottles.

It was a lengthy process. Our duties could take us past midnight before we were at last ready to ceremonially pour in the ounce of wine needed for that night.

I learnt a lot about red wine, principally that I liked it! You could measure its quality by its percentage of alcohol. This was easily determined from the little labels on the bottle proclaiming that was it was from the southern side of a sun-kissed valley, infused by virgins, equal to twenty standard drinks, and, if consumed all at once, with or without Stilton, you would either drop down dead or sleep for a month. Perfect. Cheers.

Occasionally, we would take a bottle back to his cabin to celebrate the success of our labours. It was there that, even in my inebriated state, I noticed, by channelling my inner Sherlock Holmes, that the proudly displayed framed photo of him with his wife and two children on the trip to New York was different from the photo of the family displayed on the way back to Europe. He looked the same, but the wife and two children did not.

He explained he had two separate families: one in Southampton and one in New York, each unaware of the other. What a glutton for punishment. But he was not without a sense of propriety. He would switch the pictures before docking so the right family was on display for their family reunion. After fifteen years of juggling this questionable double life, his ship also fell victim to the airlines and was now destined to be scrapped and made into razor blades.

Now he had a problem. Which family would he live with? He fretted over this decision for several crossings. His normal cheer sank to deep depression and on the last voyage, he found his solution. In the exact middle of the Atlantic, and at midnight, he hoisted himself over the stern rail and fell to a watery grave. He was a really a great friend who helped me hone my chess skills and taught me to appreciate classical music. Much as I mourn his loss, an odd part of me hopes that when he jumped, he took a bottle of red and a slice of Stilton with him.

Midnight was always a common time for people to commit suicide on ships. Many would leave their shoes on the boat deck before they jumped. One passenger on *Elizabeth* was considerate enough to leave his watch and passport in his shoes: a clear clue for later identification. It makes for faster and easier roll-checking on disembarkation. A crew returning to its home port does not like to be delayed.

Not all drownings are intentional. Leaning over the stern rail at night and looking straight down into the boiling wake can have a hypnotic effect. If you watch it for long, you may become susceptible to the ocean's beckoning call. I don't believe in legendary singing sirens, but leaning further out, you may find yourself literally drawn into the swirling water. If you're on deck at night and on your own, don't do it. It is not a sailor's myth.

While not necessarily feeling suicidal, it was obvious to all of us that our lives were to change. With passenger shipping in such big trouble, was it time to 'swallow the anchor' and abandon the sea? Shore jobs were beckoning in booming industries in America and sea life seemed to have little future. I decided the *Mary*'s last transatlantic crossing would be mine as well. I didn't jump the rail. I just decided it was time to move on.

Looking back, I was young and stupid. Now I am old and stupid. But I shouldn't have quit when I did. I should have hung on for just a few more years.

For the Queens were not dead; in fact, they were just beginning. Passenger shipping boomed. Cruising took off in spectacular fashion and far from ships disappearing from the seas, they dramatically increased in both size and number. Cunard continued to play an important part in this and today has every justification for laying claim to having the best ships in the world.

Not only was *QE2* completed, but she sailed successfully for thirty-nine years under the Cunard flag and gave birth to a succession of further Queens. It was a case of the Queen is dead: long live the Queen.

2

WHAT'S IN A NAME?

CUNARD'S ROYAL LINEAGE of ships came about due to a quick-thinking, crafty ploy by none other than the King of England. He wanted to score brownie points with his wife. Even kings must do that. But, in doing so, he broke the long-established tradition of, in its day, one of the most important companies in Britain.

Cunard had always called its ships names ending in the letters 'ia'. The first ship was the *Britannia*, which in 1840 first started puffing her two side paddle wheels across the Atlantic at a stately 9 knots. Cunard's following ship names were borrowed from Roman provinces, so we had *Lusitania, Mauritania, Aquitania, Carmania, Coronia* … you get the idea. Even a one-eyed, left-footed, hairy-bottomed orangutan can see the name *Queen Mary* in no way fits with this tradition. Ponder the reason for a moment and then we will come to it.

But first, we must point out, although a trifle pedantically, that *Queen Mary* was not, as often thought, the first Cunarder ever to be named after a British queen. That honour goes back all the way to a queen who died in 1230. Her name was Queen Berengaria. She was the wife of, wait for it, sound trumpets, roll drums: Richard I.

His Majesty was popularly known as Richard the Lionheart. But he was never lionhearted enough to bring his wife to England. Queen Berengaria mostly lived in France and is believed to have never set foot on British soil. And this was before Brexit.

Roll forward six centuries. As the spoils of the First World War, Cunard won a splendid liner built in Germany in 1912 called *Imperator*. This was some payback for the Germans using a U-boat to ruthlessly torpedo and sink Cunard's *Lusitania*, despite the fact that she was carrying a full complement of civilian women, men and children. In deference to the Germans (whose borders, come Oktoberfest, I like to cross) they had taken out ads in newspapers to say they would do this if *Lusitania* sailed from New York. But sail she did and sunk she was.

So now compensated with *Imperator*, the company might have thought of naming her after Queen Victoria. But to put Her Revered Majesty's name on a former German ship might have been considered a bit off. Not cricket, old chap. So, they settled on *Berengaria*. After all, she was a Queen and fitted the 'ia' requirement. The only small problem was nobody could remember she had ever existed.

Come 1934, when Cunard began constructing what was billed as the greatest liner ever built, it now made perfect sense for their naming thoughts to turn to Queen Victoria. This was a queen very much revered by her people. She reigned through the Industrial Revolution and died in 1901. They still make movies about her.

But to use a queen's name, Cunard had to win the blessing of the Palace. One of the directors of Cunard, Lord Royden, was a friend of King George V, and was charged by the board to secure the royal consent. When out with the King doing a spot of grouse shooting, as you do, Royden seized his chance.

When the King asked how the building of the new Cunarder was progressing, Royden said it was all going well and the company wanted to name her after 'the most illustrious and remarkable woman who has ever been Queen of England'.

Quick as a flash, the wily King, grandson of Queen Victoria, said, 'That is the greatest compliment ever made to me and my wife. I shall ask her permission when I get home.' His wife, of course, was Queen Mary.

So that was that. Lord Royden was certainly not game enough to cough discretely and say, 'Actually Sire, I was referring to your grandmother.' So, *Queen Mary* it now was.

Poor old Queen Victoria missed out. It was another seventy-three years before Cunard finally named a ship after her. Commonly portrayed as stern-faced, old Queen Victoria was inclined to sniff and declare she 'was not amused'. However, historians whisper, despite her severe appearance, on a personal level she was a game old bird and did like a little fun. Discreetly, of course, particularly so with her gardener. And her Indian advisor. Oh dear, she must have been human after all.

Of course, since this naming controversy first emerged as a rumour in the 1930s, Cunard officials respectfully, loyally and steadfastly denied it. Being such loyal subjects, they would, wouldn't they?

Another story put about claims that Queen Mary herself was present when the naming issue came up and jumped in to say she would be delighted to have the ship named after her. Both versions come from a 'reliable source' and it is possible that the second happened after the first. You can take your pick, but I believe in the credibility of the first story. So there.

Three decades after the launch, when I joined *Queen Mary*, I was given an official version that the naming issue came about due to the British Government forcing a merger between Cunard and its rival White Star Line in 1934, as the government could not afford to subsidise both. While all the Cunard ships ended in 'ia', White Star's ships ended in 'ic'. Such as *Olympic*, *Britannic* and, of course, dare we mention it, *Titanic*.

For some reason or another, since 1912, that is one ship's name that's never been used again. True, a larger than life Australian mining billionaire, Clive Palmer, whose large figure echoed the size of both big ships and his impact on Australian politics, claimed in 2013 he had contracted with the Chinese to build a replica to be called *Titanic 2*.

Before it even floated off the drawing board, that one also sank, along with Clive's own fortunes. A Chinese entrepreneur subsequently announced he would go ahead with the project, but nothing happened. In 2019, with his fortunes revived, Clive is again talking up the idea and, as he is a maverick, and a persistent one at that, who can tell what will happen? It is not a completely mad idea, as the public still seems to love stories of the *Titanic* and it is just possible we will see it in 2021.

Anyway, the official explanation was that the merged companies couldn't agree for new ships' names to end in 'ia' or 'ic'. They settled on the double no-win-we-all-lose situation by opting for a completely new naming system. There's skilful diplomacy in action for you.

If Cunard had planned all along to name their new ship *Queen Mary*, then they should have been better prepared when it came to the highly predictable issue of trying to register a name. There were already two *Queen Mary* ships on the British Register of Passenger Shipping. And the British Board of Trade was not prepared to accept another.

SUPERSTITION IS SAILOR'S DREAD

One of the hairiest and strongest superstitions of the sea is that it's bad luck to change a ship's name. Heed no lesser authority than Long John Silver, who said, 'What a ship was christened, so let her stay.'

Tales abound of ships being renamed in a moment of folly only for them to suddenly meet a tragic, watery end. Legend has it that when a ship is christened, its name goes into the great Ledger of the Deep. This is meticulously maintained by none other than the bearded, gym fit, trident-wielding, sometime budgie-smuggling King Neptune himself. And you can't slip anything past that sea god of the deep.

So convincing other shipowners to relinquish their names was not going to be an easy task. However, as luck would have it, the first ship was relatively easy. That was owned by the Colonial Government, so an edict was issued and with a stroke of the clerical pen, that was that. They had never been to sea anyway.

But the other was a Scottish-owned passenger steamer on the Clyde in Scotland. And one thing is for sure: the English can't boss the Scottish around.

This *Queen Mary* was owned by a canny lot trading as Williamson Buchanan Steamers Ltd. Engaged in a competitive tourist trade, they had no wish to just hand over the name to anyone, least of all to an English company.

It wasn't exactly the Battle of Culloden all over again, but Cunard Chairman Percy Bates had to go cap in hand to Scotland and plead his case to E.W. Macfarlane, his opposite number at Williamson Buchanan. E.W. proved somewhat reluctant to relinquish the name to the big boys from England. It was only after pressure was brought from other members of the shipping world that Macfarlane accepted that his own ship should be renamed by adding the roman numeral II after the *Queen Mary* name, thus leaping ahead of her time by sixty-eight years.

Exactly what other inducements were needed, history does not reveal. However, Cunard did donate a very fine portrait of the Queen to be permanently hung aboard that *Queen Mary II*. They do love an English Queen up there.

After the liner *Queen Mary* retired in 1967 and was removed from the British Registry of Shipping, the Clyde steamer, having been spared the sudden watery grave, dropped the *II* and reclaimed her original name. Neptune was well chuffed.

Interestingly, like her big sister, the steamer too has been preserved. After many years serving as a pub moored on the Thames embankment, she is now berthed in Glasgow, while the original *Queen Mary* is a hotel ship in Long Beach, California.

One final point on the naming issue, and then I promise not to mention it again. When King George married Mary, her name was May. There had not been a previous monarch called May and it was British tradition to change a new queen's name to that of a former monarch. That's the trouble with marrying royalty. They are not content with just changing your surname; they have to rename everything. Why? Because they can.

Now, Queen Victoria, cantankerous old devil that she was, had let it be known that she certainly did not want her daughter-in-law, or any other queen for that matter, named after her, thank you very much. So, for the coronation, May could not be named Queen Victoria II, or Queen May. Which is probably just as well, as a massive liner called *Queen May* somehow doesn't have quite the same regal ring, does it?

By now you will be relieved to know that when it came to naming their next ship four years later, Cunard was in for a much simpler time. As Queen Mary had launched her ship, in 1938, Cunard invited Queen Elizabeth to launch her namesake. And in 1967, her daughter, Queen Elizabeth II, launched *Queen Elizabeth 2*. Simple. Phew.

There the Cunard royal lineage might have ended, but for a small group of people with a remarkable vision. We will get to this. But, as a direct result, defying the pundits, Queen Elizabeth II has been kept busy by Cunard for decades. She was back again in 2004 to launch *Queen Mary 2*, which fittingly enough, at that time, was the largest passenger ship ever built.

The return of this new Queen to the waves was so warmly received that Cunard pressed on to build more ships. In 2007 the long-living Queen Elizabeth II delegated the launching of another new ship, *Queen Victoria*, to Camilla, the wife of Prince Charles and the Duchess of Cornwall. This was something of a controversial decision as sentiment in Britain was still running high over the death of the prince's former wife, Diana.

In 2010 the Queen was back again to launch the new *Queen Elizabeth*. Spanning from 1938 to 2010, the Queen is the only person who was present at the launch of all three Cunard *Queen Elizabeths*. Altogether she has launched four Cunard ships, which have all successively sailed over the years from 1938 to the present day.

3 BUILDING PROBLEMS

IT'S ALL VERY WELL coming up with the grandiose idea of building the biggest ship in the world but putting it into practice presented many new problems to solve. The starting point was simple: to claim the title, she had to be 1,000ft long. And, on that modest basis, in 1926, the design team set to work.

Two years later, the drawings and the model tank testing of various hulls in simulated rough-sea conditions had progressed to the stage where costings could be made. That was where they hit the first snag. A bit like designing your first home.

The estimated costs sent Cunard directors reeling. It was going to max out their credit cards. So, back to the drawing board for some cost savings. With a little ingenuity, by 1930, the company was ready and brave enough to place the building order with the famous Scottish John Brown shipyard on Glasgow's Clydeside.

Now the real trouble started. Just like your first housing loan. Firstly, the insurance costs were so high that no insurance company would agree to cover it. Then it was discovered that before the huge ship could enter service they had to find somewhere to park her. Modifications would have to be made to docks both in Cherbourg and in New York City.

On top of this, so that the ship could be serviced each year, there had to be a big enough dry dock in the terminal port of Southampton. And there wasn't.

The docks at Southampton were owned and operated by the Southern Railway Company, which ran the passenger and goods trains from London to the docks. The company had just completed extensive remodelling and was incredulous: 'What! You want us to dig a hole more than 1,000ft long, 124ft wide and 40ft deep. And then reinforce it with concrete? All to service just one ship a year? Pull the other one.'

While no legs were pulled, this battle raged on. Tenaciously, over a seven-month period, the Cunard board surmounted other obstacles. There was the insurance for such a ship. No one wanted to touch it as the risk cost was so formidable. Eventually, the British Government agreed to cover the insurance costs above that of a normal ship. This required a special Act of Parliament. And you know how easy that is.

When it came to providing piers big enough, Cherbourg was cooperative, but New York was markedly less so. Finally, with Cunard threatening to leave New York City and operate from the rival port of Boston, they conceded. Couldn't let those tea-chuckers get all the business.

Queen Mary 2 *was built in a dry dock where she could be floated out, unlike the first* Mary, *which was built on a slipway and then launched into the sea. (Courtesy Stephen Payne)*

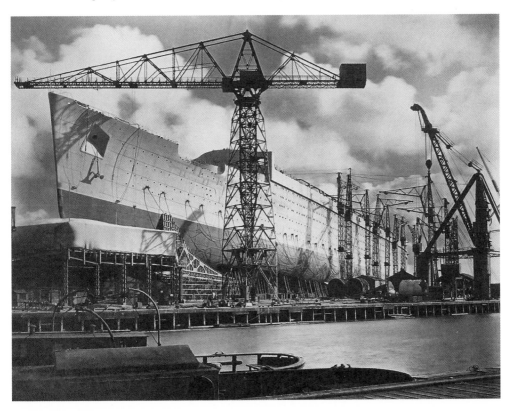

(Public Domain)

The same tactic was tried on Southampton docks, with less success. Finally, as with New York, Cunard threatened to operate the new ship from Liverpool. Southampton was succinctly told, 'No dry dock, no ship.'

Still they wavered, but the pressure was on. Cunard would not place its order for the ship to be built until the dry dock issue was resolved.

The government was watching closely as the building of the ship was going to bring major relief to the massive unemployment problem in the Glasgow region. Now everyone was waiting on Southampton docks, which was continuing to dither around. A public outcry forced the government to step in and resolve the crisis. It did this by making a special development grant for the dock project.

On 1 December 1930, Cunard was at last able to sign the shipbuilding contract and the first hull plate was immediately laid of what was labelled Job No. 534. That the ship would be eventually called *Queen Mary* was a secret closely kept for the four years it took to build her.

THE NOT SO GREAT DEPRESSION

Twelve months later, 80 per cent of the hull plating had been riveted into place. But Cunard was in deep financial trouble. The depression was biting hard and with dramatically reduced freight and passenger traffic on the North Atlantic, the company ran out of money. Staff took wage cuts, and directors too. Imagine that. But still the company could not go on paying for the build. Notice to stop work was called.

Right in the middle of this terrible depression, 13,000 people were immediately sacked: 3,000 at the shipyard, plus another 10,000 across the country who were working on the project in some capacity.

For two years, No. 534, the pride of Britain, sat rusting in the shipyard. Clydeside families were going hungry, ill-clad, often barefoot and struggling to survive on meagre rations. Still the government held back. All the while, Cunard's rival companies overseas were being supported by their governments. There was no such help in Britain.

The Prince of Wales was urged by the local Clydeside Member of Parliament to come and see the poverty problems for himself. He did. Horrified by what he saw, in another intervention by the Royal Family, he spoke a few stiff words to the British Government. Eventually, the government, still kicking and screaming, but seeing future knighthoods vanishing into oblivion, was forced by public opinion to make a loan. However, it was on the condition that Cunard and its even more financially troubled British rival, White Star Line, were merged into one united company for the transatlantic trade battle.

In March 1934, Parliament passed the bill and seven days later work on No. 534 restarted. Britain breathed a collective sigh of relief.

Never before had a ship been built such as this. The hull was comprised of steel plates, some 30ft long and weighing more than 3 tons.

Two thousand portholes and windows were cut into the hull. The ship had four propellers, each 20ft in diameter. The rudder weighed 80 tons. Twenty-four boilers, fuelled by oil from tanks that could hold 75,000 gallons, provided the engine power, while 4,000 miles of electrical wiring took the power from seven turbo-electric generators to 30,000 light bulbs and twenty-two elevators.

The ship had twelve decks and her hull was divided into 160 separate watertight compartments. Compare that to *Titanic*'s sixteen watertight compartments. Lessons had been learnt.

To finish off, it was all held together with 10 million rivets weighing 4,000 tons and 70,000 gallons of paint. There, you couldn't sink that. Or is it a miracle that it can actually float?

These images from Cunard's historical collection show the company's bid to convey just how big their new giant ship was in relation to other modes of transport of the day. (Cunard)

THE FORWARD FUNNEL of the "QUEEN MARY" IS 70 FEET IN HEIGHT FROM THE BOAT DECK. (A FOOT HIGHER THAN THE EGYPTIAN OBELISK IN CENTRAL PARK, NEW YORK CITY) THE DIAMETER OF EACH FUNNEL IS 30 FEET AND WOULD PERMIT 3 MODERN LOCOMOTIVES, PLACED ABREAST, TO PASS THROUGH, OR TO ENCLOSE THE HULL OF THE FIRST CUNARDER. THE "BRITANNIA."

THE MAIN ENGINES of the "QUEEN MARY" GENERATE APPROXIMATELY 200,000 HORSE POWER OR EQUAL TO THAT of FIFTY MODERN PASSENGER LOCOMOTIVES (EACH 4000 H.P.)

CROSS-SECTION VIEW of the MAIN ENGINE ROOMS

THE SAME POWER IS EQUAL TO THAT OF FORTY LARGE FREIGHT-HAULING LOCOMOTIVES (EACH 5000 H.P.)

65 PULLMAN SLEEPERS WOULD BE NEEDED TO MOVE THE 2075 PASSENGERS WHICH THE "QUEEN MARY" CAN CARRY ON ONE TRIP ~ 15 COACHES WOULD BE NEEDED TO MOVE THE CREW, ~ COMPARED TO

The 200 PEOPLE THAT WERE PASSENGERS AND CREW ON THE FIRST CUNARDER, "BRITANNIA"

CHRISTENED – NOT NAMED

It was Wednesday, 26 September 1934, when King George and Queen Mary arrived at the dockyard to perform the launching ceremony. It was the first time royalty had launched a passenger ship and a very different protocol was called for. As it was September and in Glasgow, surprise, it was raining.

The Royal Party unbent sufficiently to let it be known that the formal dress code of the day could be relaxed: the people could wear their raincoats. Wasn't that nice? They must have been the first of the modern royals.

Up on the launch platform, suitably sheltered of course, Queen Mary, before a quarter of a million people, stylishly cracked a bottle of champagne across the port bow and sent the massive liner sliding down the slipway for her first taste of salt water. The 'champers' was from Australia – in those days, the British supported their empire.

Thus No. 534 was christened (note, not 'named') *Queen Mary*. There was none of that political correctness nonsense about naming and christening in those days. And after all, the ruling British Monarch was the titular head of the Church of England and his subjects were always singing to the Almighty to look after him. Amen to that.

At the launch King George proclaimed, 'It has been the nation's will that she should be completed, and today we can send her forth, no longer a number on the books, but a ship with a name in the world, alive with beauty, energy and strength.'

Fitting out was done on the Clyde and in March 1936, *Queen Mary* – that's the ship, not the Queen herself – was towed by tugs to the now completed Southampton dry dock. There she spent three months for final finishing before her first transatlantic sailing in May.

With her three funnels, the *Mary* was a very imposing sight. Each stack was 38ft in diameter and the two whistles on the forward funnel were more than 6ft long. Each one literally weighed a ton. If you were standing forward on the top deck when she blew, you not so much heard it as felt it. The sound carried for 10 miles, which is just as well as that was the distance it took her to stop.

MIRROR, WHO'S THE FASTEST OF THEM ALL?

On her maiden voyage, fog prevented the *Queen Mary* from wresting the coveted Blue Riband for the fastest crossing set by the French liner *Normandie*. Cunard did not want another *Titanic*. Yet one month later, she crossed in three days and twenty-seven minutes at an average speed of 30.14 knots. This shaved five minutes off the *Normandie*'s record. The Blue Riband was hers, but the battle was on.

In response, the *Normandie* opened her throttles and reclaimed it. After a slight modification, the *Mary* gained some speed and wrested it back again and then went on to hold it for many years. This was helped by the *Normandie*, while berthed in New York City, conveniently bursting into flames. However, Cunard maintained it was not interested in anything as mundane as recording the fastest crossing.

They claimed their only reason for the *Mary* doing a faster crossing was to give the engines a good workout as a test to help build a sister ship. Oh yeah? But to their credit, Cunard never advertised or promoted the fact it held the record: word of mouth did that.

Queen Mary immediately proved a great success and didn't have enough berths to meet passenger demand. Buoyed by this, Cunard proceeded apace with the building of a sister ship that could leave New York at the same time as the *Mary* sailed from Southampton.

The design process for the new ship, *Queen Elizabeth*, was easier and did benefit from seeing the *Mary* in practice. For further ideas, Cunard sent a spy posing as a passenger aboard the *Normandie*. He said he was a grocer, but, with some of the detailed, technical questions he was asking, he must have raised a few French eyebrows. Why would a seller of sacked potatoes want to know the inside measurement of the aft smoke stack?

With an eye to votes, the British Government, basking in the glory of *Queen Mary*'s success and not wanting to see unemployment return to the Clyde, this time were much more forthcoming with financial help.

The building contract was again signed with John Brown's shipyard and at the end of 1936 work began on Job No. 552. While there were 3,000 welding and riveting at the shipyard, the need for components, furnishings and fittings spread many other employment opportunities across Britain. Altogether, a quarter of a million people were employed on the project.

This time the naming was a simple matter for Cunard. They merely selected the name of their current queen. The Queen herself did the christening honours on 27 September 1938. The King had to cry off at the last moment as he felt he couldn't leave London at a time when Britain was on the brink of war with Germany.

Queen Elizabeth was more than up to the job as when the vital moment came, and the tide was at its peak, the ship unexpectedly started to slide on its own down the slipway. The assembled officials were caught unawares, but the Queen quickly pressed the champagne-bottle release button, just in time to break against the last part of the bow.

It is important for tradition – and you don't get more traditional than seafaring Brits – to call the name of the ship before she hits the water. Quick as a flash, the shipyard chairman, Lord Aberconway, leaned across, whispering a plea to get out the vital words. She calmly replied she had already done that. And indeed, she had. It was just that the splendid gold and silver microphone especially made for the event hadn't picked it up. But she quickly said it again. Believe me. Go google.

In film coverage of the event, she can clearly be heard twice saying, 'I name her *Queen Elizabeth*.' So, the ship was well and truly christened and presumably doubly lucky.

The Queen's daughter, Princess Elizabeth, who later also become a dab hand at launching liners, was there with her sister Margaret and had a good view of the excitement. Princess Elizabeth was aged 12 and at one point she was held high by the shipyard director, Sir Stephen Pigott, for a good look at the ship named after her mother.

The *Elizabeth* looked quite different from the *Mary*. She was 12ft longer and with only two funnels she had one less than her sister. This was made possible by improved engineering. This also allowed the giant and imposing ventilators used on the *Mary*'s top deck to be eliminated to give more room on the sports deck. The *Elizabeth*, quickly and affectionately renamed by the crews as the *Lizzie*, also had finer bows with a more pro-nounced rake, while the foredeck was fitted flush with the bow. A massive V-shaped steel breakwater on this deck protected the ship from being swept by any huge, head-on seas.

At 118ft, she had the beam of the *Mary*, but her gross tonnage of 83,673 made her 2,436 tons more. Those of us working on the *Mary* considered this a very minor play at one-upmanship and that we were a better and friendlier ship with a better staff attitude. And hell, we had the extra funnel.

Lighter wood panelling interiors were used on the *Lizzie*. On the *Mary*, we thought this looked el-cheapo modern bling and cold. Oh yes, there was great rivalry between the crews of the two ships. Although we had to confess the officer accommodation was better on the *Elizabeth*.

I made only two voyages on the first *Queen Elizabeth*. On my first day I am touring the public rooms and noting with a critical eye that the stewards are much more casual than their counterparts on the *Mary*.

Look, there are two just chatting together, and over there is one looking very bored and even leaning against a column with a silver salver dangling lackadaisically from his arm. Tut-tut, you would never see that on the *Mary*.

I am joined by the regular entertainments officer who, with tongue in cheek, asks what it's like to be on a real ship. I sniff and say his stewards are sloppy and describe some of the things I've seen.

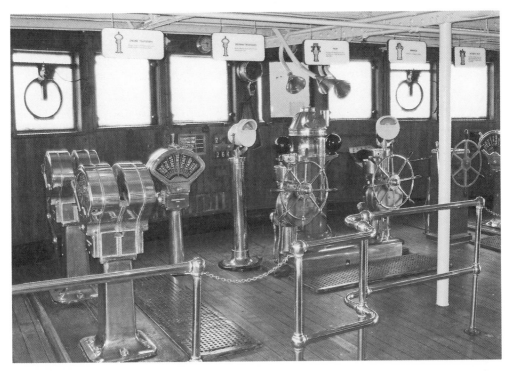

The bridge of the original Queen Mary *with its large steering wheels and engine telegraphs is a far cry from the* Queen Mary 2 *of today with its air-conditioning and its banks of computer screens. (Paul Curtis)*

The bridge of QM2. (Cunard)

'Where?' he demands. I turn to point them out but now they are all bolt upright and bustling about. He laughed, and we shared a joint realisation that it was because they didn't know my face and I was not in uniform. Now we knew what passengers sometimes saw, but we never did.

However we tried to construe things on the *Mary*, we couldn't argue against the fact that the *Elizabeth* was the biggest ship in the world and was now Cunard's flagship. This allowed her captain to be named Commodore of the Fleet and fly the special swallow-tail commodore's pennant from his ship's masthead. Damn, that hurt.

But due to a dramatic change in world events, the battle to be the fairest of them all on the Atlantic was to be delayed. The two ships were not able to engage in their dual Atlantic crossings for another eight years.

Captain Aseem Hashmi aboard the current Queen Elizabeth *uses a new system for piloting where roles and not ranks are used. The roles are from left to right: Co-Navigator, Navigator and Operations Director. The bridge is coloured blue as in spacecraft and operating theatres, as this colour has been found to keep everyone alert. (Courtesy Captain Aseem Hashmi)*

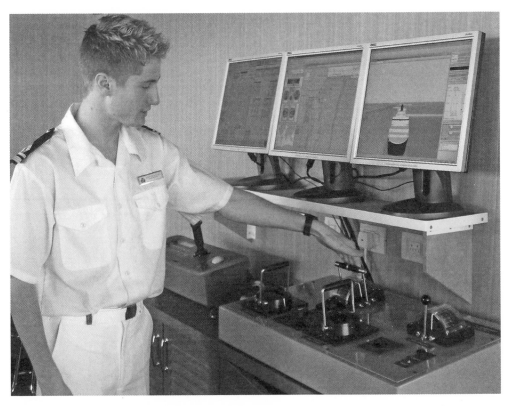

Aboard Queen Mary 2, *Jeremy Saltonstall demonstrates how a computer is used to simulate a docking procedure without the use of tugs. (Paul Curtis)*

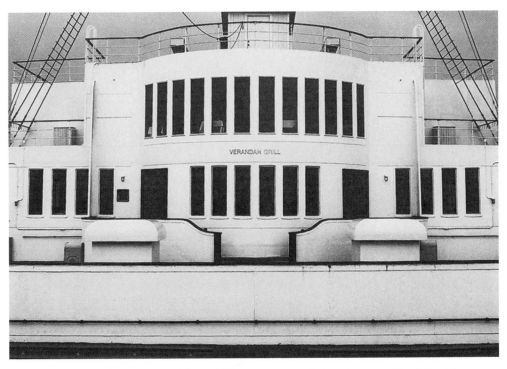

Although very old, the first Queen Mary *still has very strong design elements. (Paul Curtis)*

The large stately funnels of the first Queen Mary *needed stays rigged for greater strength. (Paul Curtis)*

The indoor pool on the first Queen Mary. *(Paul Curtis)*

Ranch pool on the new Queen Mary. *(Paul Curtis)*

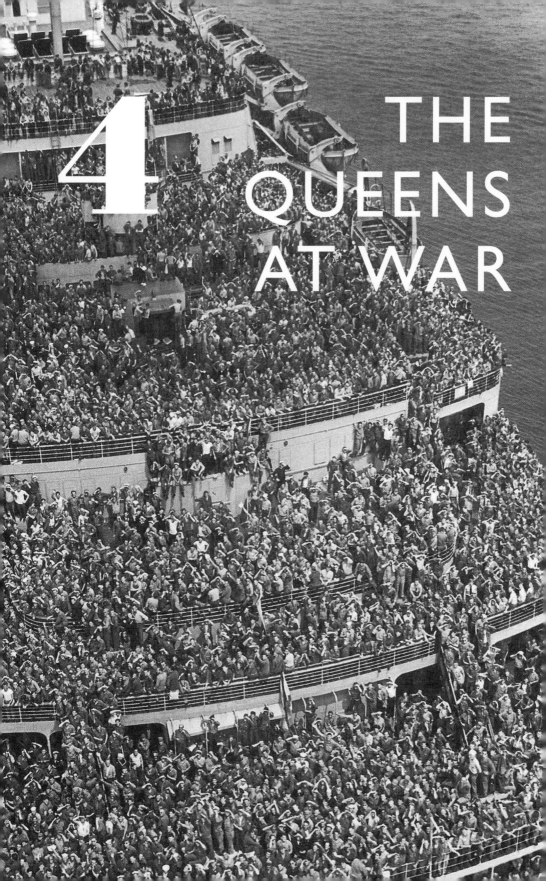

4
THE QUEENS AT WAR

SEPTEMBER 1939: The Second World War is declared. *Queen Mary* was more than halfway across the Atlantic on her way to New York. With strong memories of the U-boat mercilessly torpedoing the civilian liner *Lusitania* in the last war, you can imagine how eagerly every German U-boat commander was scratching a very itchy trigger finger.

The *Mary* sprung into immediate evasive manoeuvres, altering her course to steer a confusing zigzag pattern as she raced to the safety of New York's war-neutral harbour. Future scheduled transatlantic crossings were cancelled. She remained tied up in New York with just a skeleton maintenance crew.

Six months later, she was joined by her unfinished sister ship, *Queen Elizabeth*. For her maiden sailing from England there had been no hoopla.

The dignitary, the cheering crowds, the media and the fire tugs spewing huge plumes of water high into the air were all absent. Instead, *Queen Elizabeth* slunk out of her Clydeside fitting-out basin under 20 tons of camouflage grey paint and a dark cloak of secrecy and, look over your shoulder, diabolical deception. Remember, America was still neutral, but Nazi spies were everywhere.

However, the *Elizabeth* is too big to miss and as she navigates down the Clyde to the open sea, the word gets out and onlookers crowd the riverbanks. With only a skeleton crew aboard, everyone thought she was bound for the Southampton dry dock to load the furnishings and other supplies already sent there. But this was just a cunning ploy and a subter-fuge by the Brits to fool the Germans.

And it did. Waves of Luftwaffe aircraft were seen flying all over the Southampton approaches, but there was no big new ship to bomb. Bother. For instead of sailing south as everyone surmised, *Elizabeth* was sailing west, flat out for America.

This didn't only take the Germans by surprise, it also gave the crew the shock of their lives. It was only on the day of sailing that the captain opened sealed orders from Winston Churchill directing him to head at full speed directly for New York.

With no idea this possibility was in the offing, at the last minute the workmen and crew were given a chance to leave. But British spirit came to the fore. With not even a toothbrush or a change of clothing, most opted to stay and thus suddenly found themselves off to the States. So, that night, they were to be a bit late home for dinner. For many, it was more than a year before they could get back to Britain.

FROM LUXURY LINERS TO TROOP SHIPS

To Cunard's distress, by the time *Elizabeth* was a day out of New York, the news of her escape had leaked out. As she was docking, huge crowds swarmed the piers to see her for the first time. This was not good news for Cunard as sabotage agents were everywhere. They were to be blamed for the fiery death of the great French Liner *Normandie* while she was meant to be nice and secure in her berth in New York.

It is possible that arsonists started the fire, but it was human stupidity that sunk her by having the fireboats pour water all over her until she filled up and rolled over.

New York now had the world's two largest liners in its port and tensions were running high. What to do with them? There was some talk of selling the two ships to the Americans, but Winston Churchill had other ideas. Merchant navy ships flying the red ensign flag of Britain can be called up for war service. This was now being done with a vengeance, so why not add the Queens to the duty list?

Some merchant ships were converted to armed cruisers; others had their superstructures altered to disguise them as warships and were given the unenviable task of acting as decoys.

With only a fake means of defence, they were sitting ducks. Who would want to sail on one of those? Some were converted to mine sweepers, while others had their hulls especially strengthened so they could be heavily armed with guns to warship standards.

This last option had been rejected as Britain wanted to indicate the Queens were designed for peace and peace alone. But that had no effect on Hitler. On the heads of both ships, he put up a bounty equivalent to £50,000. In those days, that was a very tidy sum of money indeed. For a U-boat commander it would be like winning the national lottery. But with much better odds of a win.

The North Atlantic approach past Ireland was known as U-boat Alley. The Queens' captains were very expert seamen, but as the prized targets for both the German Navy and the Luftwaffe, it is little short of a miracle they escaped the sinkings and devastation taking place around the world.

The British decided that risky as it was, the two Queens would make ideal troop ships as they could carry whole divisions from one war front to another.

The first step was to fit both Queens with antimagnetic coils to protect against mines. The idea here was to explode the mines before they got close enough to damage the ship. Hem.

They also had a mine-sweeping system, which consisted of streaming a torpedo-shaped device on strong cables either side of the ship. The theory was the cables would cut the anchor lines attaching the mines to the sea bottom and cause them to float to the surface. There, says the manual, they can be safely exploded by a rear-mounted gunner. The game of Russian roulette comes to mind.

The Queens' main weapon of defence was their speed, but as a last-ditch defence, they were also fitted with cannon and anti-aircraft missile launchers.

For the conversion work to troop ships, the two Queens were first sent to Cape Town and then, for further work, on to Sydney, Australia.

The first to arrive Down Under was *Queen Mary*. In her camouflage grey, the locals nicknamed her the Grey Ghost. In spite of all the attempts at secrecy, you can't hide a ship of that size in the middle of Sydney. For that, the ship was too big and Sydney too small.

Standing on the *Mary*'s bridge, Captain Harry Gattridge heard a local tourist boat announcing to the world over its Tannoy speakers, 'On our starboard side, ladies and gents, the greatest phantom you have ever seen. For why? Because you may think it is the *Queen Mary*, but officially it ain't!'

Typical Aussie humour! I live there now, and I can tell you that, eighty years later, when they are chucking shrimps on the barbie, it is much the same.

On another wartime visit to Sydney harbour, Captain James Bisset took exception to a tug blowing its boilers immediately below the *Mary*'s bridge. It was sending up voluminous clouds of sooty black smoke into his pristine chartroom.

Too much for Bisset to take, he grabbed a megaphone, marched to the wing of the bridge and yelled down to the skipper of the tug 80ft below, 'Do that again and I will spit down your funnel and put your bloody fires out.'

Some versions of this story, which may appear in less refined publications than this, might say it wasn't spitting down the funnel that Bisset was threatening to do.

By the spring of 1941, the conversion work was finished and a total of 11,600 Australian soldiers were taken on board the two ships for transfer to the battlefronts.

This could not be done for both ships at the same time, as Sydney harbour did not have the docking or anchoring room – a situation which, to Australia's shame, still exists today. This meant *Queen Elizabeth* had to be sent to Hobart to await her turn. It was during this shuffling, and with Japanese submarines reported in the area off Sydney Heads, that on 6 April 1942, the two Queens met at sea for the first time.

RUNNING THE GAUNTLET

Living in constant fear of being torpedoed, the Queens began their troop transport work. One day, in the middle of a vast and empty ocean, a radio officer rushed up to the *Mary*'s bridge, waving a signal and excitedly calling to Captain Bisset that Japanese radio was reporting the *Queen Mary* had just been sunk.

Bisset was calm. He paused, thoughtfully scanned the peaceful horizon and noted they were still afloat. Turning to the messenger, he dryly remarked, 'Better keep it under your hat and not tell the troops. It might worry them.'

On another occasion, on a run to New York, *Queen Mary* passed five lifeboats filled with sailors from a torpedoed British ship. As there were still submarines in the area, the captain of the *Mary* could not risk the lives of the thousands of troops he was carrying by stopping to make the rescue. With heavy regret, he pressed on. However, as he passed, he did signal that he had reported their position to other ships so that they would come to their aid.

On one of the lifeboats, left bobbing in the wake, was the son of the *Mary*'s chief purser. Watching his dad speeding on, he ruefully said to his mates, 'There goes the big bastard!'

Fortunately, the following day they were picked up by an American ship and all were saved.

During the war, it was humour, albeit often grim, that kept everyone going. Once, in the Red Sea, *Queen Elizabeth* passed the battleship of the British Navy called HMS *Queen Elizabeth*. Up went the signal flags with a laconic one word greeting: 'Snap'.

Neither Queen ever had to fire her guns in anger and both survived due to their unmatched speed. However, *Queen Mary* did manage to sink an anti-aircraft cruiser. Unfortunately, it was one of her own protective convoy.

Passenger deck space was limited when the Elizabeth *was serving as a troop ship.*

The *Mary* was approaching the Scottish coast with American troops aboard where she picked up her escort fleet to help protect her from the U-boat- and Luftwaffe-infested area ahead. The escort consisted of four British navy destroyers and the anti-aircraft cruiser HMS *Curaçao*.

The flotilla was steaming in zigzag formation when the coded signal went up to change to zigzag pattern number eight. This meant the *Mary* would turn twenty-five degrees starboard and run for eight minutes, then fifty degrees to port and so on with other variations while the escorting flotilla manoeuvred out of the way in pre-planned synchronisation. The *Mary* was travelling faster than the flotilla could manage and, essentially, in a few seconds of error, one ship zigged when it should have zagged.

Well, you can guess what happened. The *Mary* crashed at full speed into *Curaçao*, slicing her in half and quickly sending her to the bottom. Tragically, aboard the cruiser 329 lives were lost.

To make things worse, again the *Mary* could not stop to help. She would have been a sitting target. And, with an entire division of thousands of GIs on board, it was far too big a risk to take. Instead, with a gaping hole in her bow, she limped on to Scotland, leaving two navy vessels to pick up the *Curaçao* survivors.

While the Royal Navy gets the accolades it so richly deserves, it is not altogether appreciated just how dangerous it was for sailors on merchant ships. They had to go about their duties, with little or no protective armament, while under the constant fear of being blown to hell, drowning in oily seas, or swimming with sharks. It tends to spoil your day.

During the Second World War, a total of 3,180 merchant ships were sunk, often in freezing waters where there was little chance of survival. Of the 150,000 seamen serving in the British merchant navy, 35,000 lost their lives.

As troop ships, the Queens could, and did, carry up to 15,000 troops and crew. To this day, this still stands as a record for the number of people carried on a single ship. One Queen captain alone, James Bisset, during the war years, transported more than half a million people.

It wasn't comfortable. Both ships had been stripped of all their finery and the great public rooms crammed full of makeshift sleeping cots made of stretched canvas. In the lofty-ceilinged public rooms, the cots could be stacked as high as six tiers. Falling out of the top one was not a good start to the day.

With so many aboard, the troops' combined weight could endanger the safety of the ship when she began to roll in a heavy sea. For this reason, the ship was divided into three zones and the troops wore colour-coded badges which strictly confined them to their allotted station and thus ensured their weight was evenly distributed about the ship.

Captain Bissett noticed that the troops would stagger in the direction of the ship's roll, thus accentuating the severity of it and running the risk of toppling the ship over. After consultation with other captains and the British Admiralty, it was decided in winter, when the seas were stormy, to reduce the number of troops carried on the North Atlantic run to 10,000 and to use only the lower bunks.

NOW HEAR THIS

Mealtimes were organised with military precision. Those who maybe now are reading this aboard a Cunarder, while perhaps taking high tea to the gentle accompaniment of a string orchestra, might pause and reflect on the differences between troop ship and cruise ship passenger life. Compare this with the official wartime GI Standing Orders for the two meals a day:

When going to the mess each man takes with him his field mess kit. The mess lines are formed by the compartment officers five minutes before the scheduled sittings no later. These lines are held in the corridors adjacent to the main staircase, but do not proceed down until told to do so by the Military Police control officers. When the troops do descend, they do so under MP control, two lines to starboard side and two lines to port side.

Once inside, troops proceed with maximum speed to seats as directed by the messing officers and stewards.

Tables must be filled to rated capacities, otherwise no seats are left for the last men to enter the mess hall. Once seated the troops remain seated, and their food is brought from the galley by the KPs [kitchen police].

As soon as a soldier has finished his meal he gets up from his seat, empties his garbage in the garbage pan at the end of the table, and then proceeds to the aft end of the mess hall, taking his mess-kit with him. The troops exit in six lines, two through each of the three exits. Troops leaving the mess hall through the centre door are routed by MPs to mess-kit washers on A and B decks; those leaving through the side exits are routed to mess-kit washers on D deck.

At the washers, the mess-kits are washed first in hot, salt water spray, then a bath of hot, soapy salt water, and finally in a clear salt water rinse. The soap used in the saltwater wash is a non-lathering type, therefore few suds are visible. In washing the mess kits, troops must use the minimum time necessary and at all times must keep moving. After leaving the mess kit washers troops return immediately to their quarters, seeking directions from the M.P.s as to the best available route.

There were six sittings a day of forty-five minutes each for the two meals and they never ran late. And you thought choosing between first and second sitting was difficult.

In another memo, GIs joining *Queen Mary* on their way to England were given some handy hints on how to deal with the British by the US Army Special Service Division. They said: 'You are better paid than the "Tommy". Don't rub it in. Play fair with him. It isn't a good idea to say "bloody" in mixed company as in Britain it is one of their worst swear words.

'To say, "I look like a bum" is offensive to their ears. For the British this means you look like your own backside. The British are beer drinkers – and they can hold it!'

There's your true Brit for you. Note that nothing was said about seducing young ladies with nylon stockings and racing them off to the States. Anyway, this advice was the basis of a new era of Anglo-American relations.

Without air-conditioning, the Queens went where they were never designed to go, voyaging across the tropics and calling at theatres of war around the world. They carried troops from Australia to Europe, from the States to Europe, to the Middle East and back to Australia again.

The crossing of the equator in overcrowded and non-airconditioned ships was arduous and even caused some of the men to die during the voyage. Return trips were less crowded and thus a little more comfortable. For these voyages, they acted as hospital ships and carried home both the wounded and prisoners of war.

Together, the two Queens managed to transport more than a million troops without firing their guns and Sir Percy Bates claimed that the service of the Queens shortened the war by a whole year. Sir Winston Churchill is also said to have agreed.

This shortening of the war proved a saviour. It was only at the very end of the war that the Germans developed the ability to rain down their V1 and V2 rockets on English cities. This ruthless bombardment was totally devastating and to save Britain from total collapse, the war in Europe was won only in the nick of time.

If the Allies had lost, think how different the world would be today. We would have had a whole series of self-aggrandising, bigoted leaders who would have ruthlessly abused their own people, spent money they didn't have, twisted the media and feathered their own nests. We were lucky to escape that one. Or did we?

CARRYING OFF FAIR MAIDENS

With the long war finally over, the Queens still had some final duties to perform. In 1946, *Queen Elizabeth* was busily engaged in helping carry home the troops from their war zones. The *Mary* took on the huge task of bringing back to the States all the spoils of war the US forces acquired in Europe. This mostly took the form of the local young ladies they had married and in many cases the babies that had resulted.

Fast talking and equipped with that good supply of nylon stockings, so highly desired yet virtually unavailable in wartime Britain, opportunistic GIs seduced many a fair English lass away from the resentful local menfolk and persuaded them into marriage and moving to the United States.

'Humph,' muttered the jilted British, holding their pints and sitting on their bar stools. 'It wasn't the charm of the Yanks that won those maidens. It was those damned nylons.'

Altogether, *Queen Mary* brought 12,886 GI brides to the States and their waiting husbands. She also carried a similar number for the Canadians.

These voyages caused great scenes of excitement when arriving at New York's Pier 90. Thousands of eager husbands and their families swarmed, cheering and shouting, to the dock. The piers would be so crowded, it was difficult to move. To get the brides reunited with their right man was a military operation. The wives were disembarked in alphabetical order and placed in holding cages, until their man could be found to collect them. This gave the women their first early taste of marriage.

The Queen Mary *in her 'Grey Ghost' wartime colours.*

It could take more than a day for the last couple to be reunited. However, at this stage, at least the women were not kept in their cages overnight.

While the Americans compensated neither the British Government nor Cunard for transporting the troops or their brides, Cunard ultimately benefitted for generations. With families divided by the Atlantic, many a voyage has been made to the other side for family reunions.

During my time on the Queens, returning couples often brought with them their beautiful daughters, who in turn repeated the cycle by marrying someone from the other side. And so it goes on. To this day, Queen Mary 2 frequently carries families honouring this generational tradition.

PUTTING THE SHIPS BACK TOGETHER

With their war work finally finished, in September 1946, Queen Mary was sent off to be restored to her former glory, while Queen Elizabeth was sent back to the Clyde for her long-delayed, proper fitting out.

While both ships came through the war unscathed, they were not unscarred. While much of the decor had either been removed or bordered over, the Queens were covered in dirt and grime. Thousands of GIs had whiled away their time at sea whittling their initials into the teak railings. This was not considered vandalism, but a part of the ship's history. A few small sections were cut out and preserved. The rest of the rails were shaved down to their traditional smooth finish.

The task of reinstalling and reassembling the Mary's fine furnishings and artwork was a giant jigsaw puzzle. While some furniture had been stored in New York and Australia, thousands of pieces had been stored in England, but as Southampton had taken a terrible pasting from the Luftwaffe, as a precaution against a direct hit on one main storage facility, the fittings were housed in places scattered around the New Forest. It took ten months to collect everything from the towns and villages, such as Brockenhurst, Lyndhurst and Lymington, and put it all back into place.

Everybody is an art critic, but none more powerful than the chairman of the company. On a ship's progress inspection, he looked at two new paintings installed either side of the ornate first-class lounge fireplace. After studying them for a few seconds, he sniffed and said to the accompanying art manager, 'You know what you can do with those.' Not sure quite how to proceed, the manager sought more detailed instructions. Came the retort, 'Give them to the blind school.'

On 31 July 1947, *Queen Mary*, eight years after she had begun her war service, repainted and sparkling in her former colours, left Southampton on what was promoted as her second 'Maiden Transatlantic'. Not many ladies get to make that claim twice. Although, no doubt, some have tried.

An equally sparkling *Queen Elizabeth* left New York for Southampton and mid-Atlantic the two ships crossed for the first time. Finally, the Atlantic ferry service had begun. It was to last for twenty more years.

When conditions were right, in mid-ocean the ships would pass within 1,000ft of each other. Passengers would line the rails to wave and cheer.

In the *Mary*'s first-class dining room was a 24ft by 15ft map with moving crystal models of the *Mary* and *Elizabeth* showing their relative positions as they steamed back and forth. A similar map was displayed in the *Elizabeth*.

It was quite a complicated clockwork mechanism and frequently gave trouble. However, unless the ships were in the right position, one of the *Mary*'s captains would flatly refuse to take dinner in the dining room.

He had endured years of making do under wartime conditions. But now there was peace, and everything on the Queens had to work perfectly. He had no hesitation in showing his displeasure for anything that didn't. That was the sort of British 'stuff' that embodied and built the Cunard legend.

5
THE
TRANSATLANTIC
YEARS

INSTEAD OF BATTLE-HARDENED TROOPS, the Queens were now carrying celebrities, rich businessmen and tourists. The officers and crew had to swiftly amend their approach to the new passengers. These were not conscripts on their way to war, but service-demanding, rich and successful passengers able to choose between a number of competing shipping companies.

Interviewed at the time by the *New Yorker* magazine, Commodore James Bisset was asked if it was not something of a let-down to command the *Elizabeth* on a peacetime run. With his dry humour, Bisset answered, 'Oh aye. But not so bad. We've no bombs and torpedoes, but we do have the passengers.'

With their Royal Navy Reserve war training, the Queens' captains had become accustomed to ruling their crews with old-style military discipline. Right at the outbreak of the war, one captain assembled in parade-ground style his scruffy but startled civilian stokers, stewards and deckhands. Surveying them with a militaristic, disapproving glare, he barked, 'Shape up! You're in the Royal Navy now and don't you forget it.'

While most captains and their senior officers were quickly reminded of the social arts needed for fare-paying passengers, some were a little slower to change their treatment of staff and crews.

I know, as I was one of the first officers told by head office to work in passenger clothing, a concept that one of my captains did not like. He used to refer to me as 'the civilian'. I never dared retort, 'Aren't we all?'

Adding to the feeling of still being on Her Majesty's Service was the fact both Queens carried the coveted prefix of RMS, so the full correct name of our ship was RMS *Queen Mary*. This stands for Royal Mail Ship.

In pre-email days, the mail was the most important form of communication and the carrying of the Royal Mail contract was highly prestigious and only awarded to the most reliable ships. Those vessels not entrusted with this royal blessing carried such ordinary prefixes as SS for steam ship, MS for motor ship, TS for training ship and even QSMV for quadruple screw motor vessel. Maybe Cunard will name one of its new smart-phone enabled ships as the SMS *Queen*?

Along with the mail, the Queens were entrusted with the safe transportation of gold and silver bars by the ton, numerous priceless paintings and very valuable jewellery. While the *Lizzie*'s strong room was deemed impregnable, the most priceless item ever carried was kept under the captain's bed.

This was Lincoln Cathedral's copy of Britain's Magna Carta. Ratified by King John in 1215, it is considered the keystone of British law, rather as the constitution is regarded in the United States. Drawn up by the Church as an agreement with the ruling monarch, only four copies were made. In it, the Crown promises the protection of church rights and to keep barons from illegal imprisonment. It also called for access to swift justice and imposed limitations on feudal payments to the Crown. If only!

The Charter became a revered part of English political life and was typically renewed by each succeeding monarch. In doing so, there were frequent updates to cover the numerous breaches arising from political conveniences of the day.

Before the war started, the precious Lincoln Cathedral copy of the Magna Carta was carried by *Queen Mary* to America for exhibition in the British Pavilion at the 1939 New York World Fair. This was fortunate as, with the outbreak of war, the Luftwaffe began peppering English cities with bombs, particularly around the Lincoln area as it was home to many British Command airfields. After the exhibition, rather than send it back to Britain, it was thought wiser to keep the precious and ancient document in the impregnable Fort Knox.

Returning it to Britain after the war symbolically signalled that the long struggle was over, and it was a big event. Arriving in New York, an armed guard delivered it on board the *Lizzie* with the captain himself in attendance.

When it came to push it into the largest safe in the strong room, it was discovered the packing crate was half an inch too long to squeeze inside the steel door. Bugger. Commodore Bisset scratched his head and then decided the safest place on the ship was under his bed. He thus became the first man in history to sleep on top of the Magna Carta.

Bisset was one of the most popular captains in Cunard history and, although he ran a tight ship, his British crew were not afraid to risk a joke at his expense. Once, when deep below decks making an inspection tour with an apprehensive section crew team beside him, he stretched up his arm to run his fingers along the top of a beam. Examining them, he found them covered in dust and tut-tutted. As the group moved on, he held back and surreptitiously slipped a penny atop the beam. A trick he had no doubt learnt from an earlier Cunard captain, Bill Irvine. A week later, making another inspection, he paused in the same spot and stretched his arm to the top. The accompanying staff party watched closely. When he opened his palm, he discovered he was holding two half-pennies.

An engine room on the first Queen Mary.

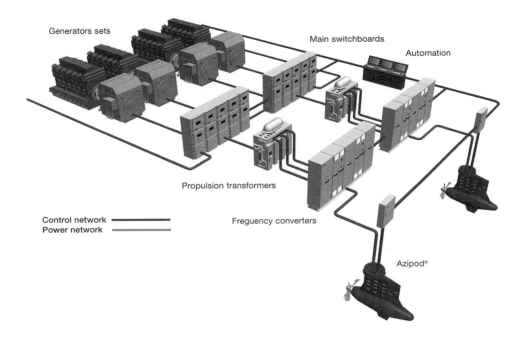

Generators sets

Main switchboards

Automation

Propulsion transformers

Freguency converters

Control network ————
Power network ————

Azipod®

The Engine Control Room on the new Queen Elizabeth. *(Courtesy Captain Aseem Hashmi)*

DIFFICULT DOCKING

With their weekly sailings, the Queens dominated the North Atlantic for three decades. Held in almost reverent awe by travellers, they held the lion's share of what was irreverently referred to as the ditch-crossing trade.

To be appointed the captain of a Queen was a great honour and the pinnacle of a seagoing career. Only the best made it and manoeuvring the great monster-sized ships into their docks took great skill. Before the later invention of rotating propeller shafts and bow and stern thrusters to move the ship sideways into a dock, as many as six or more tugs were needed.

During a 1953 industrial dispute in New York, in a bid to bring Atlantic trade to a standstill, the tugboat crews went on strike. However, captaining the world's biggest ship, Donald Sorrel was undeterred by the absence of tugs. Although it had never been done before by a ship of this size, the captain was determined to keep to his schedule and tugs or no tugs, nothing was going to stop him from delivering his passengers to New York.

Judging wind and tide to perfection, and before a ghoulish crowd of 2,000 and the incredulous tug crews, he carefully and successfully brought the *Elizabeth* alongside Pier 90 unaided. Ha! In later tug strikes, other Cunard captains proved they also could repeat Sorrel's feat.

Crews loved to boast of their captain's skills. Once, when the *Elizabeth* was dropping a pilot in rough conditions off the coast, the small pilot boat was having trouble manoeuvring close enough to the towering liner for the pilot to disembark. Watching the repeated attempts of the pilot boat to come alongside the slowly moving ship, the exasperated bosun manning the boarding ladder hailed the bridge. 'Pilot boat wants to know if you can move a bit closer sir!'

The classic writer, Mark Twain, was enamoured with Cunard and wrote: 'The Cunard people would not take Noah himself until they have worked him through the lower grades and tried him for ten years. It takes them about fifteen years to manufacture a Captain, but when they have him manufactured to suit, at last they have full confidence in him.'

For all their skill, Cunard captains were required to take mandatory retirement at age 63. However, for many years it became Cunard tradition to never announce a captain's final voyage. This is because, in 1936,

Sir Edgar Britten announced his retirement only to collapse on the *Mary's* bridge just after his final docking in Southampton. He was rushed to hospital but died the next day.

SICK OF THE SEA

When the first *Queen Mary* was built, the designers thought a ship that size would never roll. Wrong. Roll she did. Like a pig! Passengers went skittling from side to side and down the long alleyways like bowling balls. Urgently, the company fitted hand rails so at least they would have something to cling onto.

After the invention of stabilisers and their fitting in 1957, the ship settled down to be more comfortable in rough seas. During the sea trial to test the installation, the sea was dead flat. But the captain found that by working the stabilisers up and down he could rock the ship quite violently. Observing the puzzling sight of the huge *Mary* violently rocking in dead-calm water caused a nearby vessel to become concerned and rush over to offer assistance.

The stabilisers were found to reduce the roll by 75 per cent and therefore were also fitted to the *Elizabeth*. But I will tell you a little secret. They both still rolled. The dining-room chairs were anchored by a rope into a deck bolt. The tables were fitted with edges that could be raised to stop plates sliding onto the deck. By Cunard stewards, these were called 'twiddlies', but they are more commonly known as fiddles. The waiters also used to dampen the tablecloth to minimise plates and glasses sliding about and, to ease digestion, the menu was changed to more basic fare.

I've spent most of my life on the water: big ships, small ships, big boats, small boats. I've been seasick on them all. After six consecutive years on ships, I was as sick the day I got off as the day I got on.

True, like most, I settle down in a couple of days, but if the ship cruises for three or more weeks in calm seas, the minute she starts to roll again, the sweat breaks out on my brow and … ugh.

Compounding my problem, on the *Mary* was a directive from my cruise director not to deviate from a pre-scripted welcome-aboard speech, which I had to deliver to passengers in the lounge immediately after their first dinner.

I was to tell them persuasively, very seriously, straight faced, ne'er even a hint of humour or roll of eye, that the ship was far too big, far too heavy, and far too wide, for anyone to ever, ever have been seasick aboard the RMS *Queen Mary*. My boss was some sort of psychology expert.

We would be just entering the washing-machine waters of the Bay of Biscay, when with a feverish brow, a face whiter than starched cabin sheets and with microphone clutched in a white-knuckle death grip, I would deliver this nonsense. All the while, the ship would be heaving and rolling with the guests desperately hanging onto the edges of their chained-down drinks tables. This type of psychology may have worked for some passengers, but it sure didn't work for me.

Compounding matters, I had to detail the amount of food we took aboard for the four-day crossing. For 3,000 passengers eating 10,000 meals a day, the nausea-inducing list included: 77,000lb of fresh meat, 27,000lb of poultry, 11,000lb of fish, 50,000lb of potatoes, 33,000lb of fresh vegetables, 70,000 eggs, 22,000lb of flour, 11,000lb of sugar, 14,000 gallons of milk, 2,000lb of cheese, 1,000 boxes of assorted fruit, 3,000qt of ice cream and 3 tons of butter. Oops, I've forgotten the salt and pepper. By this time, my stomach would be rumbling like an ill-balanced washing machine.

Then would come the drinks list: 20,000 bottles of beer, 6,000 gallons of draught beer, 15,000 bottles of wine, 5,000 bottles of spirits and a partridge in a pear tree. Under fair weather conditions, the thought of the drinks list would brighten me considerably.

I would next ask the men to volunteer for help with the washing up: 16,000 pieces of cutlery and 200,000 pieces of china and glass.

Then, like a sexist pig (but it was the 1960s!) I would ask for lady volunteers to help with the laundry: 30,000 sheets and 31,000 pillow cases. And don't forget the 6 miles of carpeting to vacuum. But there were never any volunteers, just like home really.

One passenger, feeling unwell and obviously missing the welcome-aboard talk, took to her cabin. She asked her stewardess if it could be seasickness?

Toeing the company line, the stewardess said, 'Don't worry madam, this ship has stabilisers.'

The lady asked for two stabilisers. Unfazed, the stewardess scurried off and came back with two seasickness tablets.

So yes, we did occasionally have seasick passengers. Sailors like to say that at the first stage of sickness, you think you are going to die. A little while later, you reach the second stage: you wish you had.

One fellow sufferer was the writer Paul Gallico. Aboard for one very rough crossing, he became inspired to write *The Poseidon Adventure*. It was made into a film and for the rough-sea shots they used a model of the *Mary*. However, I can assure potential cruise passengers who might have seen it that Hollywood typically took the story miles too far.

There are some good things about storms at sea. Neither the storm nor the sickness lasts longs and, if you can make it to the dining room, you can just about sit anywhere you like.

Cures for seasickness? Oh yes, I've tried them all: tablets, injections, ginger root, acupressure wrist bands, dry biscuits, horizon staring, eye of newt, hair of dog, you name it. Only one I can guarantee: go sit under an oak tree.

Oddly enough, after a long time at sea and first landing back ashore, it can feel as though the earth is moving. That can make you so sick you want to get right back on the ship.

Returning to shore life takes some conditioning. At sea you are always pushing objects on shelves away from the front edge to stop them vibrating off. It becomes a hard habit to break and you're likely to find yourself doing the same when home. I discovered it drives mothers mad.

HAPPY SEA DOGS

The *Queen Mary* and *Queen Elizabeth* were the most successful and profitable team in the history of the North Atlantic. Through the 1950s passengers booked months in advance to secure a berth. The rich and famous flocked to be photographed embarking and disembarking from the famous ships.

The *Mary*'s maiden voyage had set the tone for the Queens by making a series of live broadcasts from the ship by famous British bandmaster Henry Hall with the virtuoso harmonica player, Larry Adler. During the crossing, pop singer Frances Day performed a song written especially by Henry Hall called 'Somewhere at Sea'. It became the ship's signature tune and, if you want a trip down nostalgia lane, you can still find the recording on YouTube.

Frances Day arrived at the wharf in true celebrity style. Along with a team of press photographers, she brought along her own chickens. She was determined to have fresh eggs for breakfast every morning.

After this made the news, it began a trend for passengers to bring their pets on the crossings. Special dog kennels were installed, and an exercise deck was set up complete with, for the convenience of British dogs, a lamppost. American dogs were also catered for: they had a fire hydrant. Cunard still follows this tradition.

Arriving at quayside, seeing the towering ship, and then boarding past the line of bellboys was an impressive experience. When comedic actress Beatrice Lillie came up the gangway, she looked around at the huge purser's square and asked, 'What time does this place get to England?'

The Queens were the biggest and most technologically advanced ships afloat. The British were so proud of them, one reader even huffed off a letter to *The Times* querulously asking why the menus were printed in French. 'Seeing they are all British ships, built and partly subsidised with English money, would it not be out of place to have the menus in the good old English language?'

Partly due to the role the Queens played for the United States during the war and partly because they were the biggest and best, most Americans assumed that the ships had to be theirs. That attitude used to annoy the hell out of us Limeys.

Learning that this was not so, a Texas billionaire, travelling to Europe on the *Elizabeth*, thought it a matter of United States patriotic duty to put this to rights. He told the commodore he wanted to buy her, but he shook his head and said she was not for sale.

'Why not? I can afford it,' demanded the Texan. The commodore murmured, 'Well you see sir, she is part of a set.'

But America was not to be outdone. In 1952 the American liner *United States*, although a smaller ship, stole the Blue Riband from the *Mary* with an average speed of 35.59kt, a 4.5kt increase on the *Mary*'s best record. This caused great jubilation amongst the *United States'* crew. Arriving in Le Havre, they spotted a British warship moored immediately astern of them and began calling out jeering remarks. Such opportunities are a bit hard for a sailor to resist.

But back came the riposte, 'When you get to Southampton, don't get too close to the *Mary*. In that little thing you might get hoisted aboard.'

Losing the Blue Riband caused neither Queen to lose any of their magical appeal to passengers. However, in the 1960s, on a trip back to New York on the *Elizabeth*, Commodore Donald Maclean overheard a lady saying she preferred the *Queen Mary* to the *Queen Elizabeth*. Her explanation was you get more sleep in the *Mary*.

'How come?' her companion asked. She explained when the ship had left New York for Southampton, an extra hour was put on the clock every night, whereas, in this ship they were taking an hour off every night.

'Really', exclaimed her friend, 'I thought it was the sea air making my watch lose an hour every day.'

If you are worrying about my use of the words 'in a ship', remember, that it should not be 'on a ship'. You get in a ship, but on a boat! Happy now? Funny lot, we sailors.

I SAY, OLD BOY

In my early 20s and coming from an ordinary family, I was not really up to speed on how to deal with the more eccentric aspects of some of our travelling celebrities.

On my first trip, I was detailed to join the welcome-aboard line greeting the passengers arriving on the first-class gangway. My task was to beam and flash the young ivories, proclaim 'welcome aboard' and be on hand to assist with any problems that might arise.

All was going smoothly until there was a raised voice and a tremendous kerfuffle coming up the gangway. Pushing his way to the front of a heavily loaded swarm of porters was a face I immediately recognised from the telly as that of Lord Boothby. He was a giant of a man, red faced, with a booming voice and clearly upset. And he hadn't yet even stepped foot in the ship.

Ivories vanished and replaced with concern, I tentatively moved forward only to be swept aside as he stormed into the crowded purser's square. A sea of stewards, bellboys and pursers surrounded him, but such was the commotion, I don't think any of us knew what to do.

Then the pursers' cabin door swung open and out came our majestic chief purser, an equally large and impressive figure. He spied Lord Boothby and with a matching booming voice cried, 'Stinkers old boy! Wondered what all the damn fuss was. Should have guessed. Come and join me in a noggin old fellow.' And off they went, arms around each other's shoulders. Now, to get away with that, you must have been at school together.

KEEP PLAYING

The three classes on the ship were kept separate. However, there was one daily occasion when everyone could tour the whole ship, but only under guidance. This was the early morning daily deck hike and was led by either the tourist-class or the cabin-class entertainments officer. More senior cruise staff were above this sort of activity and would remain hidden snugly in their beds.

Passengers in each class were asked to assemble in their purser's squares where they were collected group by group. With much undignified hooting of an old car horn and plenty of loud group laughter, the entertainments officer walked them for thirty minutes up and down flights of stairs and through the lounges of each class. Up on the sports deck, we put them through a series of keep-fit exercises. Great fun! Ah yes, in those days that did qualify as passenger entertainment.

At midnight, our more senior cruise staff would again seek sanctuary in their beds while the colleague who had not done the early morning deck hike would be tasked with roving all three classes to keep entertainment going for as long as there were passengers about.

It was always very noticeable that the first and second classes would be fun-loving night owls, whereas middle-class cabin passengers were more practical types that tended to drift away for an early night.

On one late shift I was on, but for a dozen or so passengers in the first-class lounge, sitting quietly with their drinks and listening to the band now reduced to a trio, the whole ship had disappeared to their cabins. It was 2.30 a.m. and I thought it now safe for me to sneak off to my own bed.

I am just drifting off nicely when comes an urgent banging on my cabin door. An anxious steward is urging me to return immediately as there is terrible trouble. He seems unable to tell me what it is, so I quickly jump into my dinner jacket, wrestle my black tie into rough position and race back up the stairs.

I slow to what I think is an unhurried and unperturbed stroll through the grand entrance into the impressively marbled lounge. All seems peaceful. The few passengers are sitting quietly chatting to each other and the band is playing softly. Puzzled, I look around. Ah, there is the problem. On top of our spectacularly white grand piano are a partially undressed couple deeply embraced in each other's arms. They shouldn't be on top of that prized piano. Oh, I see. They are languidly making love. Crikey. This form of entertainment is certainly not on the programme.

I am meant to be in charge, but how to deal with it? I look at the pianist, still hesitantly stroking the keys. He catches my eye and jerks his head for me to come over. Reluctantly, I approach. He puts his mouth close to my bended ear and whispers, 'What do I do?'

What does he do? I am stunned. I am completely out of my depth with this situation. I realise I am expected to give some form of instruction. My brain spins hopelessly. Maybe he should try a catchy Russian polka, the Radetzky March perhaps, or, possibly, *Chariots of Fire*.

Maybe that's the sort of thing I would say today, but in my misguided youth, all I can do is stammer, 'Keep playing'.

There, I sure knew how to handle that one. The band leader, a much older and wiser man than me, is looking over with some amusement to see how I would cope. Finally, taking pity, he goes to the gentleman and gently asks if he wouldn't be more comfortable in his cabin.

The amorous couple jerk their heads up, blink as though puzzled and unaware of what they were doing. Then, calmly readjusting their clothing, he helps her down from the piano and they quietly leave. I slink from the lounge and back to my bed. I pray that head office never, ever hears about that one. Oops, if they read this, they just did! But it was more than fifty years ago.

Maybe it is the motion of the ocean, or the fact that at sea we are far from the inhibiting constraints of normal and parochial living. Whichever, there is no doubt that being at sea definitely does have something of an aphrodisiac effect on some, but not all, young ladies.

It doesn't affect men. No matter where, they are permanently randy. My shipmates have reliably informed me of this. But at sea, add in a little 'star' power and all hell can break loose. The more famous, the more infamous became the ship's gossip. If they only knew what went on, it would send today's tabloids into a total meltdown.

For instance, Hollywood 1960s screen star Victor Mature was regarded by some ladies of his day as a kind of Brad Pitt on steroids. He was a regular traveller on the Queens and, with the obliging help of some swooning-inclined ladies, developed a notorious reputation. On one trip, two stewardesses went missing for two days. When the captain was informed, he ordered a full search of the ship. Just at the point when he was about to turn back to make a sea search, the news came they had been discovered happily sequestered in Mature's cabin.

After that, a notice went up in the crew quarters saying that anyone who accepted an invitation to a cabin party from Victor Mature would be instantly dismissed.

There was a sort of vague understanding that at sea, thrust together in a confined space for days with no land in sight, people might not always behave with their usual shore-based standards of propriety. On first joining a passenger ship, crews were told there were two golden rules that must be strictly obeyed. Rule one was under no circumstances and on pain of instant dismissal, never, ever interfere with the cargo. That, of course, was a reference to the passengers. Rule two was under no circumstances and on pain of instant dismissal, never, ever get caught.

This even applied to entertainments officers whose job included inviting passengers to their cabin parties and, in full view of everyone, joining the ladies after dinner to dance the night away. But the expected ratio was for us to dance with four old ladies and then just one young, attractive lady. Even then, it had better not be the same young lady all night. Damn.

These days, on Cunard that aspect of an entertainments officer's tasks seems to have been filled by 'Gentlemen Hosts'. These are older men who have been especially retained by Cunard to dance with the ladies. At first, I was vaguely uncomfortable with a role being made just for that specific function. However, I have come to accept they do fill a passenger need and, worse still, the lucky bastards can actually dance.

CHAMPAGNE SOCIALIST

Looking back, I can see how inadequately equipped I was in my young age to deal with many of the situations I encountered aboard the Queens. For instance, I am compering an afternoon function for a British consular event held aboard while the ship is docked in New York. I am also meant to be in charge to see everything runs smoothly while my superiors are off in the city having a good time.

After giving a few words of greeting, I go straight into the dancing and begin my crowd mingling. 'Bumbling', we used to call it. You would go up to a group and say 'Enjoying yourselves? Lovely day? Isn't it all marvellous fun, what? Bumble, bumble, bumble.' Nauseating, isn't it?

This afternoon one of the guests is the British Foreign Secretary George Brown. George was a former militant unionist and a great champion for the workers, but it quickly became apparent his socialist tastes stretched to a strong liking for champagne. Yes, he really is liking it, isn't he? Now he is becoming even more jovial. Hem, these VIPs sure know how to let their hair down.

I watch anxiously from the side of the lounge until the Right Honourable takes it into his head that although the ship is securely berthed in harbour, we are in fact rolling heavily at sea. Closely clutching a smartly gowned and bejewelled lady, the minister falls to the dance floor and rolls around, still tightly wrapped to his now alarmed-looking dance partner.

Golly. This is certainly a foreign affair. Looking around and seeing no senior officer, I telephone the bridge.

It was just my luck that the man I am most afraid of, the captain himself, answers.

'What do you want, boy', he barks imperiously.

'Sir, I've got a drunken shore visitor in the lounge.'

'Deal with it,' comes the stern reply. 'That's what you're trained for.'

'I can't sir.'

'Ridiculous!' snaps the captain. 'Who is it?'

'The Secretary of State for Foreign Affairs of Great Britain, sir.'

Immediately the phone bangs down. Seconds later the captain magically appears. And I had thought the distance from the bridge was at least a five-minute run, even for Usain Bolt.

The captain helped the cabinet minister to his feet and had a few quiet words in his ear. To my stunned amazement, they happily chatted away together for a few moments and then they wandered off.

Wow. How the heck did he do that? Was the captain going to put the foreign minister in the brig? I discovered the answer later. But somehow, however, I don't think that if it was me that had made the invitation to view the bridge, it would have been quite so effective.

The captain, god bless him, did come up to me later to tell me I had done the right thing.

EDUCATING ARCHIE

Another embarrassing situation arose at one evening's cabaret show. I was all set for a great treat as I was excited at the prospect of introducing a star ventriloquist and his famous puppets.

With a prime-time Sunday radio show on the BBC, Peter Brough and his puppets Archie Andrews and Daisy May were household names in Britain. A ventriloquist with a regular spot on radio? Only the English! However, 15 million people across the country tuned in every week to hear the distinctive saccharine sighing of his pigtailed, wooden doll seductively saying, 'Hello. I'm Daisy May.' In England, this had become a national catchphrase. Even more curious.

I was eager to see this famous act live and in the flesh, so to speak. After my sycophantic introduction, Peter Brough arrived on stage to his theme music, opened his suitcase and, with the whole audience leaning forward with anticipation, pulled out English children's sweetheart for us all to see for the first time. We all sighed with delight.

Well! In person, the sweet and adorable Daisy May turned out to be the most vulgar and foul-mouthed puppet imaginable. Definitely, adults only. Certainly not *Queen Mary* material. Even the seamen handling the lighting blanched.

Afterwards I could see wall-to-wall shocked faces with only a little nervous tittering coming from distant corners of the room. I hurriedly moved on to the next act.

In the excitement of making the introduction of a celebrity, I was always fearful of committing the terrible sin of giving the big build-up only to end up stumbling over the performer's name.

You couldn't be seen using notes: if they're famous, you're meant to remember who they are. And, in the intro, it is vital not to mention the celebrity's name until the very last word. The reason for this is that it's the cue the band is waiting for to immediately and loudly strike into the star's signature walk-on music. Get it wrong and you have a hell of mess.

For peace of mind, I took to writing the star's name on the palm of my hand. If I blanked out, with a flourishing arm wave, I could read it there. However, hot and sweaty under the lights, sometimes the ink could run and become illegible. More sighs. That's show business.

PIG 'N' WHISTLE

On one trip, we had Yehudi Menuhin aboard. Acting on my own initiative, I approached him to ask if he would like to play for my passengers in cabin class.

He rejected the offer and after a pause said, 'But I will play for the crew.'

This was outside of my remit, but the crew! The thought made me wince. Thinking quickly, I told him, 'Wonderful, the officers will be delighted.'

'No', he said, 'the crew: the deck hands, the workers, the stewards.'

Now, many of them were a tough but good-hearted Midlands and Merseyside lot and more into the Beatles than the classics. I paled at the thought of their reaction to a high-brow classical concert and knew I was now in over my head.

I went to my boss, the cruise director. He laughed and said, 'Good luck with that one. You'd better talk to the master at arms.'

He went on to explain it was a tradition started by Paul Robeson and often followed by other celebrities. When asked by the captain to sing, Robeson said passengers could buy seats in the Albert Hall. But he would sing for the crew in their special bar, the Pig 'n' Whistle.

The Pig is a popular name for English pubs. The odd name comes from the fact that wooden barrels of beer used to be called pigs and when a barman sent a boy into the cellar to tap a new one he was told to keep whistling, so the boss knew he wasn't drinking the beer.

This name has become traditional for Cunard crew bars. On the *Mary*, it was deep below decks, buried in the aft bowels of the ship and located right above the engine rooms. Off limits to passengers, it was an open area used for baggage handling in port. At sea, with the bags all delivered to the passenger cabins, it was an open recreational area for crew to sit about out of uniform, relax, play darts and drink from a corner bar. The crew considered it sacred ground and officers were barred and could only go there by very rare and sacred invitation.

I tried to visualise Paul Robeson in the *Mary*'s crew pub. Yep, possible. But Yehudi Menuhin! Gracie Fields had also played down there, and she too had said, 'Passengers can pay, but for the crew I will sing for nought.'

Yes, I could see Gracie would have been quite at home there. But I think it was Bob Hope who got it right when he first went down to play in the Pig. He opened up to a chorus of cheers saying, 'I've never played in a sewer before! Good evening rats.'

But for me to learn all this now was far too late and so, pressing on, I arranged things with the master at arms and then went to collect Yehudi.

To my horror, he is dressed in full concert regalia and worse still, has a priceless Stradivarius tucked under his arm. I shudder. But off we go to negotiate our way down the internal, oil-stained, slippery iron stairs to the depths below. There is no way I am offering to carry that violin for him.

The Pig is vibrating from the engines and the thumping swish of the waves along the hull. There is a raucous bunch of singlet-wearing, hairy-chested sailors playing darts, and sitting around on empty beer barrels with pints of ale. They are obviously already in a jovial mood and yelling ribald remarks to each other with loud cheers and jeers. Hem, they are having a good time. But help. How am I going to introduce him in this?

But this is the bosun's territory and he takes over by stepping up and vigorously banging a steel mug on a trestle table for attention: 'Listen up lads. We've got a gent here who plays the fiddle a bit.'

I quietly die. But with that introduction, the venerable Sir Yehudi Menuhin is on.

I can't say you could hear a pin drop: the background engines are far too loud for that. But the crew are silent and clearly totally entranced. At the end, they are cheering like mad. Phew.

At least, in my naively approaching Yehudi, I hadn't been as cheeky as one passenger, who, when in the dining room, asked Sir Yehudi to play 'Happy Birthday' for his table. Now that does take the biscuit for having nerve.

The tradition of celebrities giving a show for the crew continues to this day. I believe the all-time honour of having the most rapt and attentive audience goes to the world-famous sex therapist, Dr Ruth K. Westheimer when aboard QM2. No prizes for guessing her subject.

THE BAD OLD DAYS

While we had frequent performances by the big names working their way across the Atlantic, mostly the entertainment and its presentation were very basic. It was nothing like today's Queens with their West End-style theatres and teams of technicians sitting in glassed-in bio booths controlling rising stages, moving curtains, elaborate lighting and extensive sound systems.

The dance band was on a low stage at the back of the dance floor. A couple of scrubbed-up and smartly dressed deckhands would each man a single follow spotlight shining from both sides. Completing the setup was a stand with a detachable microphone shared by both compère and performer.

As for the ship's disco, there were no smooth-pattered DJs operating fog machines, booming speakers, rows of turntables, mixing desks and strobe lights.

On the *Mary* there was just us humble entertainments officers working what we called the disco in a small room located deep in the stern. For sound, a monster jukebox held 100 single-play vinyl records. But, in spite of its size, it struggled to be heard over the noisy engines. The mechanical change arm took a long thirty seconds to swap from one vinyl disc to the next.

For the disco party, the entertainments officer would arrive with a bag of sixpences in his pocket to feed the flashing beast. A few awkward teenagers would gyrate without partners to the music of the Beatles, Elvis Presley, Chubby Checker and the Rolling Stones. If we spied a young lady we wanted to dance with arm in arm, then we fell back to selecting *Dr Zhivago*'s 'Lara's Theme' or Sinatra singing 'Strangers in the Night.'

Another major difference from today's ships was the swimming pools. These used to be mostly located well below decks. There was no daylight, but there was more warmth and being low in the ship, the water did not slosh around so much.

The gym consisted of a small converted cabin containing a single exercise bike, a set of dumbbells and a weighing machine. It was rarely used. Not so today, as now we see rows and rows of high-tech exercise machines with crowds of people huffing and puffing away before they head off to the lavish spa facilities.

In the 1960s, while some passengers would elegantly stroll the decks, most seemed content to sit on the promenade deck in their steamer chairs, wrapped in warmed blankets, and drink their hot bouillon. At other times you could find them sitting in the lounges, or in the pursers' lobby, indulging in the favourite sport of people watching.

As an entertainments officer, part of my daytime job was to 'bumble' the passengers. For the lonely, a little chat here, a little chat there. Once the sun was over the yard arm, and we kept it very low on the *Mary*, we could ease this tortuous process for both bumbler and bumblee by buying them a drink.

There were meetings to host for various special-interest people such as Kiwanis, Masons, Rotarians, Lions, religious and ladies' groups. Of course, there was also the daily game of bridge, but in those days, an eye had to be kept out for professional gamblers who criss-crossed the Atlantic plying their card-sharping tricks for a living.

On the modern Queens, strictly controlled casinos provide all forms of gambling. Even the betting on the daily mileage run has been abandoned. Gone is the nautical chart displayed so passengers could wager on the next day's noon position. This practice was abandoned after passengers started arriving armed with portable GPS units and smart phones.

Our standard evening entertainment was the dance band with the main excitement coming from novelty dancing, such as passing the broomstick, statue dancing, where you have to freeze the moment the music stops, elimination dancing, where, for example, any couple wearing green is asked to sit down, or simply musical chairs. Exciting stuff.

My own pet hate was trying to lead the sing-song sessions. Partly because, apart from being tone deaf, my own voice sounded very similar to the ship's foghorn on a rainy day. But we all assembled dutifully in the lounge and struggled through the Cunard song book. Americans found these printed lyrics particularly helpful as they warbled through such songs as 'There is a Tavern in the Town', 'Daisy Bell' and the 'Whiffenproof Song'. I still shudder at the memory.

On one night, we would have the traditional fancy-dress competition, with its regular parade of Charlie Chaplins, Carmen Mirandas, King Neptunes, et cetera. We saw the same character impersonations each trip, probably because passengers mostly used the limited range of dress-up materials we offered.

OFF TO THE RACES

On another night, we held our own brand of horseracing. Lining up for events listed on the race card as The Queen Mary Mile, The Atlantic Steeplechase and The Ocean Stakes Handicap was our special stable of no doubt wittily named horses, such as Always in Order by Never Out of Place, Broken Window by Eva Brick Out of Space and Spinster by Hope Out of Leap Year. Let the record show that I had no hand in naming the horses. Horses in the *Queen Mary* Lounge? In fact, they were six painted, wooden silhouettes complete with numbered jockeys and mounted on small stands. Two smart sailors would move them along a green velvet racetrack marked out with furlong lines.

After passengers had placed their wagers, a lady guest was invited on stage to roll five dice. The process of rolling the dice, announcing which horse was to move and for how far, could make for a tedious process.

To get more of the genuine racetrack feel, we hatched a plan to keep the horses moving at a lifelike rapid rate. I would ask the dice shaker, always a lady, to roll as fast as she could. My hand would then immediately close over the dice, before the passenger or even I could take them in and return them to the cup for another shake. While this was being done, with an old pair of binoculars around my neck, I called the field just thrown with random numbers plucked from my fevered mind.

Perhaps remembering some of the numbers I had just glimpsed, I would rattle off the horse names in fast racetrack style. The sailors, catching the odd word, would jiggle the horses up and down the track as best they could. On the final furlong, the punters, seeing their horses still tightly bunched, would all be on their feet, stamping and cheering to madly egg on their horse.

None of us could really be sure what was happening. Cheating? I don't think so. It was still a game of chance as none of us knew who the eventual winner would be. Looking back, it was just possible that I was being naive. Could the sailors moving the horses have known and already placed their own bets? I don't think so.

This was better than the way horse racing was played on liners from a different company. There, each horse was attached to a wire running to a fishing reel held by a passenger. Six passengers, lined up in chairs on the dance floor, frantically reeled their horse to the finish to the cheers of the crowd. However, one of these passengers would have whispered advice from a friendly purser that when their horse was approaching the finish line to simply, and quickly, jerk their reel back like they were landing a fish. The selected passenger would feel honoured to get this tip, but no prize for guessing which horse all the pursers had put their money on.

LEGS ELEVEN

Every evening we would call bingo. In those days, this was done by having a small bag containing numbered plastic discs. A lady passenger would be invited on stage to shake the bag so that the MC could reach in and pull out a number to call bingo style: 'Quack-quack, two little ducks in the water; two and two, twenty-two; whichever way you look at it, sixty-nine.' Painful, wasn't it!

If their numbers were not coming out, players would frequently yell out 'shake the bag'. So, bingo was quite a raucous affair; unlike today where it is mostly played in stony silence.

In the south of England, bingo, or 'housey-housey' as the English liked to call it, was considered a very working-class game. My mother, who aspired to greater things for me, was horrified to see on BBC television one night some film of me calling bingo.

'Darling,' she chided on my next visit ashore, 'I realise in your work you may have to do that sort of thing, but really, did you have to let the BBC film it!'

The last game of the night was called 'snowball bingo', in which only limited numbers were called. If no one called 'bingo' or 'house', then the prize money would be held over and added to the prize for the next night.

On the last night, the prize money would be considerable, and all numbers were called until someone screamed 'Bingo!' As the prize money grew, so did the anticipation and on the last night passengers would eagerly rush up to the lounge in the hope of winning the big one.

On my second trip, the prize went off on the second night. 'How could you?' remonstrated the cabin class purser. 'You've spoilt the passengers' enjoyment for the rest of the trip.'

I was taken aback and couldn't see how I could do anything but call the numbers that chanced out of the bag.

'What! Don't you know anything!' he exclaimed.

He then showed me his own personally invented art to ensure snowball bingo would never go off again before the last night. It made me nervous, but I can't deny the passengers had more enjoyment his way and that passengers ended up winning a very handsome prize.

Of course, today, any harmless sleight-of-hand is out of the question as it is all electronic. And in this transition from the bingo bag, an air blower was used to fly numbered ping-pong balls in a transparent container until the air was shut off and only one at the top was caught.

However, as haphazard as this may appear, it has been known for some less scrupulous operators to put tiny pinpricks into some of the balls to make them float lower. This certainly did not happen on the tightly regulated Queens.

While bingo was not necessarily the classiest game, it was interesting to see how many celebrities loved it, as did all passengers in all classes. I guess there was not that much else to do.

TRAVELLING IN STYLE

Queen Mary could carry 711 first-class passengers, 707 cabin-class passengers and 577 tourist passengers. First-class cabins were opulently furnished, and all had telephones. The suites included a master bedroom, a smaller one for servants or children, a large sitting room and a bathroom. In such a cabin, the trip would cost fifteen times more than a humble cabin in tourist.

It was interesting to note the first-class suites were mostly occupied by politicians, celebrities, business moguls and, believe it or not, priests. The fact that clergymen were paying fifteen times the humble tourist rate could rankle.

Billy Graham, the skilled evangelist whose oratory talent made it difficult for him to find stadiums big enough for his crusades, was a case in point. Come donation time, he would passionately implore his congregations to give money for Christ. Teams of collectors, carrying large bins, would move through the stadiums collecting cheques and cash while he continued to exhort, 'Don't give change. Give not one dollar, not twenty dollars, nor fifty dollars. Give big. Give until it hurts.' Just the sort of chap you need for a meat raffle.

Well, he travelled in a first-class suite. Hem.

Seems he also loved bingo. Calling this game in the sanctified air amongst the elaborate decor of the first-class lounge in itself seemed sacrilegious. But one night I looked up and there he was, the good reverend, sitting at a table with Richard Burton and Elizabeth Taylor. At the time these film stars were both married, but not to each other, and having an affair so shocking that it had tabloid editors turning cartwheels in their newsrooms.

This was an odd grouping if ever I saw one. What's more, they were not playing just one bingo card. Each of them had three cards lined up in front of them. Smartasses. So, I decided to call the game as fast as I could. But they revelled in it and while some members of the audience were struggling with their one card, they managed to keep up. Damn. But they won nothing.

On another voyage, I lunched occasionally at the same table as the English crime novelist, John Creasey, creator, amongst other characters, of the detective Gideon of Scotland Yard. To this day, it still runs on television.

A modest and unassuming man, he only seemed to leave his cabin for meals. On the last day of the four-day passage from New York to Southampton, he amazed me by announcing he had just finished writing the novel he started on our first day at sea.

His output was extraordinary. In his lifetime, he wrote more than 600 books. That's a bit better than my output, as this one book has taken me more than fifty years.

RICH BELLBOYS

The rich and famous were one thing, but the real money earners on the Queens were the lowly bellboys. They could earn more than the captain.

Recruited at the age of 15, invariably cheeky, these smartly uniformed, white-gloved young lads used to run all over the ship paging people for phone calls, opening doors for guests and operating lifts.

Off duty, they slept twelve to a cabin on straw mattresses and were the endless victims of crew hazing. They were stripped and boot polished, locked in cupboards and sent off on fool's errands such as asking the quartermaster for some more green oil for the starboard lamp.

Traditional bellboys gretting passengers on the maiden voyage of QM2. *(Paul Curtis)*

Some initiation ceremonies were totally unacceptable and today would be front-page fodder for the gutter press for weeks and result in at least three government enquiries. Back then, they just had to shrug it off. But they had the last laugh. They earned phenomenal money in tips.

One bellboy asked the chief steward for a change of job as he felt guilty and that it was not right he was getting so much money. Passengers would press £5 notes into his hand every time he opened a door for them. During the four-and-a-half-day trip he collected £66 in tips. At the time, that put him on track to nearing what Cunard was paying its captains. This was less than £4,000 a year.

HAS THIS SHIP EVER SUNK?

One of the most tiresome aspects of working on a ship is that passengers ask the same question day after day, trip in, trip out. And that's perfectly understandable, but when you get them all the time it becomes hard to bite back some smart-arse retort that flashes through the mind, but must remain unspoken:

'Does, the ship generate its own electricity?'

'No sir, we are paying out a very long electrical cord from the pier in New York that will reach and power everything until we get to Southampton.'

'Does the crew sleep on board?'

'No madam, we have an escort barge following and at night we all get on that'.

'What do you do with the ice carvings after they melt?'

'We drink them sir.'

'Has this ship ever sunk?'

'Only twice. We had an incident in Cherbourg harbour last week, but she is okay now.'

'What time does the midnight buffet start?'

'Just before breakfast.'

'Does this elevator go to the front of the ship?'

'Only if we are sinking bow first.'

Ship's photographers get a particularly hard time. They can walk around with three cameras, a huge gadget bag, two flash umbrellas, a couple of tripods and a badge saying 'Ship's Photographer' and they get asked: 'Are you the ship's photographer?'

'No,' twiddling with cameras, 'I am the ship's wireless operator, would you like to send a cable?'

In the photo gallery, some passenger on every trip will look at the long display of photos and ask: 'How do I know which photos are of me?'

Leaving photos for processing, passengers frequently ask the perfectly legitimate question, while not seeming to realise the answer had just been given when the receipt was handed over, 'When will my prints come?'

'Sorry madam, in your case probably never, your prince is asleep for evermore.'

One passenger even rang the pursers' office to ask how to get out of the cabin. Puzzled, they asked, 'Do you have a door?'

The answer came back, 'I have two: one goes to the toilet and the other one has a sign saying, "Do not disturb."'

Another man, on his first night at sea, rang the pursers' office from his cabin asking, 'Where can we sleep? There is no bed.'

It turned out that he was confused by the plastic protective sheet placed over the bed on boarding day labelled, 'For luggage only'.

The quiz games also used to come up with some baffling answers. Asked to name the seven wonders of the world, one passenger wrote down, 'The hanging baskets of Babylon'.

It is obvious that a bit of sea air and vacation can do funny things to some brains. But that's life for you. No matter how crazy the question, we had to take a secret deep breath, smile and answer as politely as we could muster. It could be a hard life.

Which reminds me of the two ladies who met at a suburban Women's Institute meeting. They were delighted to find they were both married to sea captains. The first lady says her husband works for P&O lines. The second lady says her husband works for Cunard. 'Oh,' says the first lady, 'my husband works effing hard too.'

On the Queens, thanks to a combination of reputation and Madison Avenue advertising types, passenger expectations are very high. This has been the case throughout Cunard history, but maintaining the reputation is a hard-fought battle.

During my time on the first *Mary*, the Cunard advertising agency in New York, curse them, ran a series of advertisements boasting that the Queen's Veranda Grill was the only restaurant in the world where you could order eggs benedict at three o'clock in the morning, drink Dom Perignon and have the accompaniment of a gypsy quartet. I ask you, who would ever want to do that?

Well, at three o'clock one night, there was a frantic banging on my door by a distressed steward telling me that two passengers had just turned up in the Veranda Grill demanding the advertised breakfast.

Catering swung into action and I roused the band leader to organise some musos, donned my dinner jacket and tie, plastered on a fake smile, and returned to the Veranda Grill. But deep inside I was not happy. The time had come to let the agency know to go easy on creative thinking.

The one passenger comment that really used to get us on the Queens in the 1960s was how come there are so many Limeys on this American ship? They just could not conceive of the fact that it was little old Britain, not the mighty USA, that had built the biggest and best ships in the world.

Twin cabin on first Queen Mary.

Premium balcony, QM2. (Cunard)

Queen Mary's *first-class lounge.*

© CharlesMiller/BNPS

The first Queen Mary *had fixed propellers whereas* QM2 *has fully rotating propellers, so she can manoeuvre in any direction without tugs.*

(Courtesy Stephen Payne)

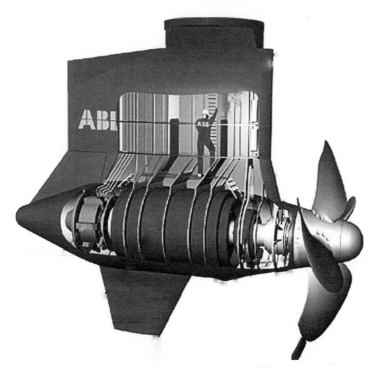

QM2's propellers are Rolls-Royce Mermaid pods and each one of the four beneath the ship is the size of a London double-decker bus. *(Courtesy Rolls Royce)*

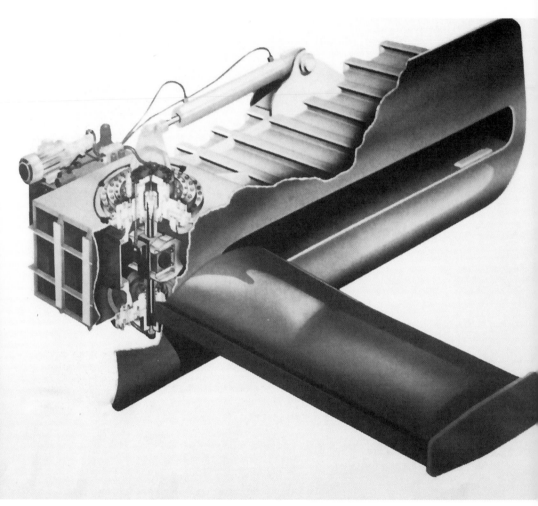

All the Queens now have stabilisers. These are like underwater aeroplane wings that slide out from the ship beneath the waterline. (Wartsila)

On the first Queen Mary, *the gym was very basic and little used, unlike the one on the new* Queen Mary. *(Cunard)*

Queen Mary's gym. *(Paul Curtis)*

ALL VISITORS ASHORE

Most of the odder questions came on sailing day when we had thousands of extra people on board. This was our busiest time for passenger handling. Before the days of modern security restraints, it was traditional for departing passengers to hold elaborate cabin parties in port before the ship sailed. Huge crowds would flock to the docks to go to the various parties and to just wander willy-nilly around the ship.

The stairways and alleyways would be filled with lost visitors looking for their host's cabin. Once found, there could be as many as twenty people crammed into a cabin meant for two. With champagne flowing, stewards delivering canapés and bellboys arriving with telegrams and flowers from well-wishers, it was total mayhem.

Come sailing time, above the ensuing din and the frequent booming of the ship's whistle, the announcements for all visitors ashore could barely be heard. Bellboys and stewards would try to round everyone up and help them find their way off the ship.

On the dockside, the visitors would form dense lines along the pier shouting across to their loved ones lining the rails. With 'bon voyage' placards waving, streamers whistling through the air, speakers blaring out 'Auld Lang Syne' and increasingly frequent deafening blasts of the ship's foghorn, the sense of urgency would resemble the half-time rush for the toilets at a football stadium.

Aboard, the stewards would now be banging gongs and the bellboys would be running and ringing their handbells all over the ship crying, 'All visitors ashore, all visitors ashore.'

There always seemed to be an unspoken competition between stragglers to be the last one off, which while convenient for would-be stowaways, would just add to the general chaos.

The ship often would sail with a few extras. When halfway down the Hudson, one lady, walking past the dining room, was asked by a steward which sitting she was in. 'Oh no,' she said, 'I will not be staying for lunch.'

While in the river, special launches would be sent out to rescue these shore visitors at their own expense. Later still, they could be put ashore via an uncomfortable ride back in the pilot's boat.

So, these were the glory days of transatlantic sailings, but by 1967, we could see it was all coming to an end and boarding would become a simple matter of calling passengers onto a plane by row numbers.

6 ON THE BEACH

THE DROP IN THE TRANSATLANTIC TRADE was particularly noticeable in winter. The seas would be icy, rough and bleak. Flying became the preferred option. Wimps!

For this time of year, the Queens began to switch to cruising. But this was a task for which they were ill-suited. Firstly, the water was not deep enough for them to berth at most popular cruise spots. The ships' architects had worked on the key factors of speed and Atlantic seaworthiness and had not considered the prospect of them being used to visit shallow-watered islands and the need to get passengers on and off by tender.

Air-conditioning? The warming system worked fine, but the attempts at cooling were pathetic. To make matters worse, the prevailing evening wear fashion of the times had ladies dressed in furs scalped off every poor animal imaginable. One cocktail party could see these ladies wipe out half the African animal kingdom.

It seems odd today to look back and think how ladies used to like to walk around with dead animals such as stoats, foxes, rabbits, otters, seals, cats, dogs and coyotes slung around their shoulders. They sure kept taxidermists busy.

Without efficient air conditioning, the ladies in their minks and furs had to swelter through the evening. Even the bravest non-conservationists would faint at the sight today. The dining room used to look like a field full of pop-up gophers.

THE DEATH KNELL

The last nail in the Queens' coffins was the British Seamen's Union. It was dominated by communist-inspired leaders. Those who weren't card-carrying communists were either naive, or, to be charitable, just plain dumb.

While the ideal of communism sounds good, most of the world has come to understand that in practice it just doesn't work. Under communism it seems the difference between the haves and the have-nots widens. The real workers can end up being taken to the cleaners worse than under capitalism.

The strike came at a time when Cunard was facing increasing competition from the airlines, strife from overseas ships running with lesser-paid crews, and the impact of the newly designed container ship on its own ageing cargo fleet.

The worst possible thing that could happen at this time was for the union to go on strike for more pay. But in 1966, strike they did.

On the first day, Captain McClean patriotically appealed to his crew not to strike due to the honour of serving on the *Queen Elizabeth*. The vast majority agreed, and the ship managed to sail. However, the strike proved all-encompassing and, along with other British ships, the entire Cunard fleet of passenger and cargo ships was soon all tied up at the docks.

Prospective travellers had to make other arrangements and consequently, thousands of loyal customers were lost forever.

It went on for seven long weeks. It was the death blow. The vast majority of British passenger ships were scrapped or sold off cheaply to overseas operators. And who bought the ships?

In many cases, it was the communist regimes. So, we ended up with the absolutely pathetic situation of former British ships cruising again, but under communist nation flags and crews and carrying British passengers. Go figure. And yes, I am still bitter.

Selling the two Queens was not an easy matter. Merely kicking the engines over was an expensive exercise. The *Mary* carried 7,000 tons of fuel and, at normal crossing speed, burned 1,000 tons every twenty-four hours. Fuelling up would max out most credit cards.

For cruising, she did not carry enough water. Her tanks held little more than 6,000 tons of fresh water, but she used between 700 and 800 tons every day. For extended cruising, desalination plants would have to be fitted.

Cunard was not keen on selling her to a rival transatlantic shipping company, as they certainly didn't want to compete in the summer season against their former ships.

The company received several proposals from potential buyers, some practical, some not. One even suggested welding the two ships together to make a giant catamaran. To berth that one, it might have been easier to bring the city alongside the ships.

Then came the winning bid from the Los Angeles city of Long Beach, which, surrounded by slurping oil wells, had the money to offer $3.5 million. The city's idea was to convert *Queen Mary* into a hotel, convention centre and maritime museum.

It was thought she would be a great tourist attraction and bring prestige to the city of Long Beach. No competition there for Cunard, so it was an ideal solution and the company signed on the dotted line.

THE SHAME ENDING

Delivering the *Mary* to Long Beach was a voyage of nearly 15,000 miles. Being far too beamy to squeeze through the needle-eyed Panama Canal, she would have to face a rounding of Cape Horn. No problem, the ship had been there before, but it was during wartime when comfort was not a prime consideration.

To offset some of the delivery costs, the city of Long Beach wanted to sell passenger tickets for the voyage. But Cunard, fearful of damaging its passenger-experience reputation, was not interested. The company did not wish to be associated with taking passengers in a non-airconditioned ship across the equator, not once, but twice. However, there were no such concerns for an American travel operator who gleefully took the job on and advertised it as 'The Last Great Cruise'.

They certainly succeeded in proving Cunard right, as due to the extreme heat and bad service from an unhappy crew, some passengers abandoned ship mid-voyage and one crew member even died.

Crowds gather to watch the final departure of the Mary *from Southampton. (Paul Curtis)*

The New Queen 2022. (Cunard)

Stephen Card's painting of the view from above the bridge of RMS Queen Elizabeth *as she crosses the mid-Atlantic with the RMS* Queen Mary. *Now one of our most celebrated marine artists, Stephen was a former officer aboard* Queen Elizabeth. *(Stephen J. Card)*

A question of scale. (Cunard)

Queen Mary's *art-deco Observation Bar. (Paul Curtis)*

One of Queen Mary's *single cabins. (Paul Curtis)*

The Captain's cabin on the original Queen Mary *was used to entertain passengers and hold staff meetings. The captains also had their own dedicated personal steward, always known as the Captain's Tiger. (Paul Curtis)*

Original two-level suite on QM2. (Cunard)

Queen Mary 2 *at sea and with cutaway interior view. (Cunard)*

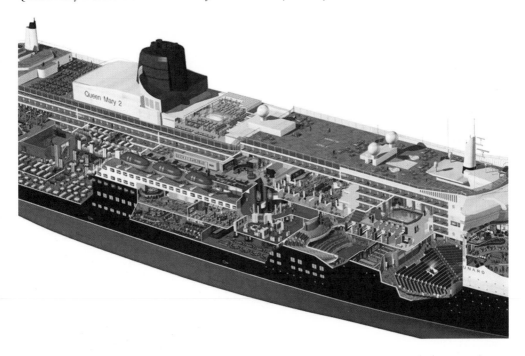

These beautifully designed wind scoops on the new Queen Mary *allow for a shortened funnel able to limbo under the Verranzo-Narrows Bridge at the entrance to New York City. (Paul Curtis)*

The Queens Room. (Cunard)

The Grand Staircase. (Cunard)

QM2's Planetarium. (Cunard)

The Britannia Restaurant. (Paul Curtis)

*Another day of adventure dawns for QM2.
(Cunard)*

Those of us on the entertainment team were supportive of Cunard's approach and did not want to be a part of what was looking like something that would have been better advertised as the cruise to hell.

And that's how, at the end of October, on this dull and dreary day, I come to be standing with a small group of colleagues at Southampton docks watching RMS *Queen Mary* irrevocably dropping all lines to her mother country.

Passengers are rushing to the rails to join hundreds of onlookers on the docks below where a Royal Marine Band is playing 'Auld Lang Syne.'

Captain Treasure-Jones leans out from his bridge for a last look and sees our little group of former staff standing forlornly on the dock. He looks grimly satisfied, even relieved, to see us standing there.

The *Mary* is making a grand but sad sight. The traditional, but longest paying-off pennant I've ever seen, is flying from the masthead. This flag signals a ship's last voyage and at 10ft for every year she has served, it is 310ft long.

As she clears the berth, we hear the other ships in port sounding their farewells with deafening blasts from their whistles. Now comes the roar of a Royal Air Force fly-past and the thump-thump of the news helicopters. As the din begins to fade, the *Mary* again hits her mighty

On a bleak day Queen Mary *makes her final departure from Southampton docks in 1967. (Paul Curtis)*

At Long Beach, Queen Mary's *bridge engine room telegraph is permanently set at 'Stop'.*
(Paul Curtis)

horns, thus setting all the other ships off again. As she passes further down the river to the Solent, both the ship and the noise gradually fade. Now there is just sad silence. But it is a spectacular send-off for a grand lady who served Britain so well.

Her delivery voyage is to take her south, past Spain and Portugal to the Azores. Then she takes a turn west for Rio de Janeiro, drops down to the Horn, rounds and heads north via Valparaiso and Acapulco.

At Acapulco, the charter company makes the mistake of taking aboard sixty journalists to cover the final leg to Long Beach. This gave disgruntled passengers all the time they needed to regale the journalists with the horror stories endured on the trip. To save money, the ship has been running on only two of her four engines. She missed the tide to enter the advertised trip up the Tagus to Lisbon. Passengers and crews sweltered across the tropics. When she reached Rio, some passengers checked into hotels to recover in air-conditioned rooms. Crew morale was at an all-time low and both service and food had been dreadful. She was not a happy ship.

The only bright reports were that the rounding of Cape Horn had been in good weather. One passenger even swam up and down the ship's pool to claim he swam around the Horn. Others paid to sit in one of the two London double-decker buses being carried on deck to Long Beach. They can claim to have rounded the Horn by bus.

Unfortunately, on 9 December, the journalists had ringside seats to witness the near riot conditions as the unhappy voyage ended with the approach to the dock at Long Beach.

Many disgruntled crew and passengers literally started wrecking the ship by throwing overboard deck chairs and anything else they could grab.

A huge greeting armada of pleasure craft out to see the arrival won some great souvenirs. However, it was a very sad ending for a ship with such a glorious history.

One journalist filed his front-page story with the headline, 'The Ship That Died of Shame'.

Despite some misgivings, I feel grateful to the city of Long Beach for taking on the difficult and expensive task of preserving the *Mary* for history. She did not prove a great commercial success. On a visit a few years after her conversion, I was invited to tour and make some comments.

The magnificent first-class dining room, with its high-domed ceiling, had been placed off-limits to day visitors and was being used as a conference centre. This was a big loss for visitors as this is one of the main architectural highlights of the ship. As a functioning lunch and dinner restaurant with a palm-court orchestra, it could have been a big draw. After all, there are around 18 million prospective customers in the Greater Los Angeles area.

Besides, with its huge columns blocking views of both the screens and the speakers, it was ill suited for use as a conference room. There were numerous, unusable inside tourist-class cabins that could have been cleared away to create a modern conference theatre with clear lines of sight.

The various marketing attempts were not successful, and the hotel operations were suspended. Various saviours and benefactors have come and gone, but in 2019 she is again operating as a hotel and tourist destination.

Maintaining the ship is a major problem. On my last visit, there were even patches of grass growing between the seams of the teak decks. It is all very sad.

However, against that, it is just wonderful she is still there. She managed to avoid the usual ignominy of the breaker's yard and ending up as razor blades. Better still, she managed to avoid the terrible fate that befell *Queen Elizabeth*.

THE WORST FATE OF THEM ALL

Queen Elizabeth was only to last another twelve months on the North Atlantic before being sold off to Philadelphia buyers for $7.5 million. In a joint venture she was transferred to act as a hotel and tourist attraction in Port Everglades. She lost her crown and became simply called *Elizabeth*. She did not fare well in the hot climate and besides, from the novelty prospective, one thing that Florida ports are not short of is a big passenger ship to look at.

She was towed to Hong Kong when Tung Chao Young bought her for US$3.5 million. He insured her for $8 million as he was going to spend $5 million converting her to a seagoing university. In a play on the new owner's initials, C.Y., she was renamed *Seawise University*.

However, the conversion work was making slow progress when in June 1972, the ship caught fire in several places at once. Fire boats came to the rescue, but, as with the ending of the *Normandie* in New York, they made the same mistake of pouring gallons and gallons of water over her until she capsized and sank. Some suspected arson or sabotage.

For some years, with her blackened superstructure still visible above the water in Hong Kong harbour, she was a heartbreaking sight. Two years later, and with no rescue possibilities, the top parts of the ship were broken up for scrap and the remains on the seabed marked on nautical charts as a hazard to navigation.

Ironically, two of the ship's brass plates showing, of all things, the fire warning system, were recovered and are now on display in the Hong Kong Aberdeen Boat Club.

The Parker Pen company seized the opportunity of using the salvage material from the *Elizabeth* to make a limited edition of 5,000 pens.

Something similar happened to *Queen Mary*, but in this case it involved just melting down a spare propeller stored near Southampton. It was made of manganese, brass and bronze, was 20ft in diameter and weighed 35 tons.

The sad end in Hong Kong harbour. (Barry Loigmangure)

An enterprising scrap merchant bought it for very little money and turned it into thousands of souvenir drink coasters that sold for very much. I know. I have some.

However, it was just a propeller, and an unused one at that. While the fate of *Queen Mary* is not necessarily ideal, it certainly beats ending up as a few Parker pens.

CHANGING FASHIONS
ON CUNARD SHIPS

1940s – Marlene Dietrich. (Cunard)

1940s – Carol Lombard. (Cunard)

(Cunard)

1930s. (Cunard)

1940s. (Cunard)

7

QE2 TURNS THE TIDE

MY NEW ZEALAND-BORN WIFE AND I are standing on the boat deck as we slip down the Hudson and watch the Statue of Liberty slide by. We are off to cross the North Atlantic once more and we are on our way to Southampton. It's my first time on a large passenger vessel for more than a decade. And this time, Cunard is not paying me. I am paying them.

It's a step I've been reluctant to take. Working on a ship keeps you busy and with the few off-duty moments you get, even our snatched relaxation with fellow shipmates becomes exhausting. Work hard, play hard.

One way or another we were always stretched as our quest to unwind from the strains of dealing with passengers was not helped by the fact that off duty we sought excessive refuge in alcohol and partying. It was a major adrenalin rush, a steely test of livers and the ability to function on little sleep. I once worked on a Dutch ship where some of us, who had to work through day and night at the end of the cruise, resorted to Benzedrine to keep going. Not good. Even so, I thought that being a mere passenger with nothing to do must be as boring as hell.

On an Italian ship I worked on, to let off a little steam, when I entered the first-class dining room for my evening meal, I would call the greeting maître d' by the most insulting names I could think of. It gets things out of the system. He would find similar ironic relief by calling me names in reply that would even make a boiler-room stoker flinch.

The challenge for us was to come up with ever-worsening greetings and never, ever use the same term of abuse more than once. As the weeks went by, our imaginations were stretched to the limits.

To make things more difficult, we never resorted to the use of profanities. For instance, yesterday I had called him a boss-eyed, buck-toothed, yellow-bellied son of a sea cook German sausage. But he had topped me with an even longer stream of carefully planned out invective.

Tonight, I am determined to better, or worsen, his last endeavour. I have planned to call him by just one word that will top all that has gone before. I pause in front of him, draw myself up theatrically and look him in the eye. I take a deep breath and then venomously splutter, 'You … you … you … Passenger!'

Startled by this ultimate abuse, he collapses with laughter and concedes I have won. He says we should abandon the game as no insult could ever top that.

Of course, we were only fooling, but after spending five years of my seagoing time cruising, as far as island hopping goes with revoltingly happy passengers, I'd had my fill.

The routine is relentless, you visit an island by day and travel to the next island by night. Just as an island is coming to life with the locals returning from work and bars and restaurants are lighting up, it's time to get back on the ship and move on.

A few uninterrupted days at sea are the only way to get to feel the true rhythm of a ship. And a transatlantic voyage is the best way to do it.

So, after a long break, here I am at sea again. But as that dreaded thing called a 'passenger'. And for our first excursion into passenger life, my wife and I have chosen what is billed and marketed as the last great transatlantic liner in the world: QE2 is vibrating gently beneath our feet.

Leaving the pier had been a quiet affair. Instead of the former thousands of relatives and friends cramming the pier waving and tearfully throwing tenuous streamer links to their departing loved ones, there is a mere handful of onlookers with hands thrust firmly in pockets. Crossing the Atlantic is no big deal now and everyone will probably be back together again in a couple of weeks.

On board, in the afternoon sun, a lively band is playing, and some holiday-mode passengers are energetically jittering the decks. This feels more like a cruise than the business of a transatlantic crossing.

An attractive deck stewardess approaches us bearing a large tray of drinks topped with a little forest of miniature, coloured umbrellas. 'Would we like a cocktail?' Why yes, indeed we would.

Turning to my wife I smirk: this is the way to travel, just like the old days. Style and largess aplenty. But the stewardess is still at my shoulder, patiently waiting. She is proffering a chit for me to sign. What? I must sign for it. Not like the old days. But, nevertheless, we soon fall for QE2's charms.

Here she is in the flesh, and in a few years she has shed her troubled beginnings and successfully assumed the mantle of being a true Queen of the seas. To our surprise, we loved her. We vowed that whenever we could on our trips from Australia to Europe, we would cross on the Queen.

We also took to cruising on her and were surprised by how much we enjoyed that. In spite of the fact that we had swallowed the anchor, we were hooked.

The birth of the new ship had not been easy. While the *Mary* and the *Elizabeth* were making their final voyages, the Cunard board had been tossing and turning enough to make the boisterous seas of the North Atlantic seem as calm as a Buddhist monk sitting eyes shut, cross-legged and chanting 'Om'.

Cunard were convinced there was still a place for them with a ship on the North Atlantic, but wrestling with the problems of what the ship should be: bigger, smaller, economy or luxury?

First, they opted to build a ship bigger than the *Elizabeth*. Code-named the Q3, the huge costs sank it before it could float off the drawing board.

Trimming the size to suit their budget, they finally settled on the design for a slightly smaller ship but with much the same passenger capacity as the former Queens. This was to become known as *QE2*. However, the building was beset with problems and rumours circulated she would be sold before ever sailing under the Cunard flag.

Adding to confusion over a new ship was an argument between the New York marketing department and the offices in London. Surprisingly, the Americans were wanting a three- or even four-class ship while the English wanted just two. Funny that, you would have thought it would have been the British that would have gone for ten.

In those days, you couldn't get a more class-conscious country than England. There was lower-working class, middle-working class and upper-working class. Close on these heels followed lower-middle class, middle-middle class and upper-middle class. Moving up came lower-upper class, middle-upper class and upper-upper class. Then we came to the lords and ladies of high society. The utmost upper echelon was royalty. In this system, everyone knew where they sat and where they aspired to be.

It was all a matter of who your parents were and where they had sent you to school. Immediately when you opened your mouth, your tongue betrayed you. God help you if you had a Midlands accent. In America, although school played some role, it was nearly all a question of how much money you had. Much simpler.

In England, having heaps of money was no help at all. In the early 1900s, multimillionaire Sir Thomas Lipton made his fortune out of his chain of grocery stores and even managed to nab a knighthood. Nevertheless, his repeated applications to join the elitist Royal Yacht Squadron were all rejected.

It only took one member to drop a black ball into the ballot box and you were out! A case of, 'I say old chap, damn feller's in trade.'

Of course, the reason the Americans wanted three different classes was all about money.

Fortunately, due to their international nature, religion is of little consequence on ships. Shipping companies tried to recognise and provide meeting facilities for all religions. This is unlike the anti-Semitic attitude Groucho Marx encountered at his posh Beverly Hills Club. He felt obliged to resign and sent a classic letter saying, 'I do not want to belong to any club that will accept me as a member.'

If you think society's attitude to race is still bad, the 1960s would have horrified you. On one crossing, our cabin-class passengers included a doctor and his wife from Nassau. On my evening rounds of the lounge I sat with them, put some drinks for them on my corporate tab and, as inevitably between West Indians and the English, we discussed cricket. With a bit of good-natured competitive sparring, we debated the all-time, best teams for a West Indies versus England test match.

Passing by every five minutes was a senior officer with enough gold braid rings circling his sleeves to make me dizzy. His intensive casting of hard looks was also making me nervous. I had been sitting with them for some time and, in my job, I was meant to keep circulating and 'bumbling' along. Reluctantly, I decided I had better do just that.

Immediately the officer came up and, to my amazement, instead of chastising me, he said, 'Well done Curtis, these days we have to be sociable with these sorts of people.'

The memory of that insight into such a dreadful, yet in those days not uncommon, aspect of human nature, has repelled me for decades. Thank heavens it represents a dying breed.

While separate class structures were economically suited to Atlantic crossings, cruising was a different matter. Cruise passengers want to feel they have the full run of the ship. As the intention was to cruise in the Atlantic off-season, this was to be an important part of any new ship design. It was decided that class segregation should be done by horizontal divisions rather than the traditional vertically straight down through the decks design.

For world cruising, rather than brave the fierce seas of Cape Horn and the regular tempests of the African Cape of Good Hope, which sometimes would be better called Cape of Little-to-no-Hope, it is best to be able to squeeze through the placid Panama and Suez Canals.

Just as a little pedantic aside, I would like to mention that the Cape of Good Hope is not the southernmost tip of Africa. It is a misconception. That honour goes to Cape Agulhas, which is another 130 miles further south. It is around here that the currents of the cold Atlantic and warm Indian Oceans meet and become, shall we say, a trifle confused. So, remember, when you reach the Cape of Good Hope and it doesn't seem too bad, don't put away your seasick tablets just yet.

Both alternative routes through the canals are restricted by their width and calls for careful attention by ship designers. Their designs need both a low draught and a narrow beam. With this in mind, Cunard settled for designer James Gardner's drawings for a 70,327-ton ship, and at 963ft in length, it was only 68ft shorter than the *Lizzie*.

With a profile more reminiscent of a super yacht than a traditional ship, she would be able to travel the Atlantic at the same fast speed as the previous Queens. However, thanks to technical advances, she would burn only half the oil used by the *Mary* and would be able to travel 8,000 miles without bunkering.

With a distillation plant for converting the sea into drinking water, the liner was almost self-sufficient. For Atlantic crossings the ship would operate with two classes but for cruising she would convert to a one-class ship.

Once again, the John Brown Shipyard in Clydebank won the building contract. This time the yard was using new tricks and had installed computers to keep track of the materials required. Out on the slipway, the riveting together of steel plates had been replaced by welding and large parts of the superstructure were built of aluminium.

The lack of riveting might have been a boon to shipbuilders, but it was the end of some sailors' favourite sport. On various nationality ships I worked on, officers chatting up young ladies at the bar would ask girls to guess the number of rivets it took to build the ship. In the case of the *Mary*, it was 10 million. The girls would gasp. Did they know that the last rivet punched into the ship was ceremonially marked by using one made of solid gold? Would they like to see it? Of course, they would. Luckily, it was in the officer's cabin. Really? I should mention that on one Greek ship I worked on there were no fewer than eight golden rivets! They were a dab hand with a spot of paint.

With this enticement, many a probably suspecting damsel would happily go to see the golden rivet. However, there were no such rivets to be found in the hull of the new ship. Ladies: forewarned is forearmed.

Building had begun in July 1965 and the unfinished ship slid down the slipway in September 1967. With the same gold scissors first used by her grandmother for the launch of the *Mary* and then by her mother for the *Elizabeth*, Queen Elizabeth II cut the ribbon and launched both ship and herself into another Royal naming controversy.

Since King George had royally mucked up Cunard's previous system of naming ships ending in 'ia', the company simply used the same name as its former ships. As was their custom, Cunard had kept the proposed name for the new ship a tightly held secret and up until the launch it was only referred to by the build number, 736.

In the sealed envelope given to the Queen on her arrival, the card simply said, 'I name this ship *Queen Elizabeth*.' But on the launching platform, Queen Elizabeth left the nomination envelope unopened and instead said, 'I name this ship *Queen Elizabeth the Second*.' In other words, intentionally or not, she appeared to have named it after herself. Queens can do that sort of thing.

But the surprise amongst the directors on the launch platform quickly turned to concern. After the Queen pressed the electronic launch button, the ship didn't budge. It just sat on the slipway.

This is a very bad omen for superstitious seamen. In reality, it was only for a few moments, but, judging by the stoic angst on the official party's faces, it must have felt like eternity. Into the stony silence, a workman on the ship's foredeck called down, 'Give us a shove!'

On the slipway and playing the crowd for humour, the shipyard director, George Parker, suited and bowler-hatted, made to move the massive ship by doing just that. As he did, the ship began to move. Wow. But it was coincidence of course. With George gleefully waving his bowler, the ship gathered speed and slid into the water. Sighs of relief all round.

Queen Elizabeth the Second is not the shortest name for a ship and although the hull was plenty long enough, writing it on the sides called for new graphics. Both *Queen Mary* and *Queen Elizabeth* had their names on the bow and stern in block capital letters. This time Cunard opted for upper and lower case and instead of the normal Roman numeral II, Cunard used the Arabic numeral 2.

This was a somewhat confusing move at the time, but it was an attempt to remove the ship from being named after Queen Elizabeth II. The problem was the ship had been built in Scotland and in that country, Queen Elizabeth II was only their Queen Elizabeth I. And heaven help any Englishman that ever inferred otherwise. Mercifully, the *Queen Elizabeth 2* dilemma was quickly solved as she became popularly known as *QE2*.

At the time of the launch, despite a new modular construction technique being used by John Brown's, the yard still had the long task of installing all the cabins, dining rooms and lounges in the shipyard's special fitting-out basin. Later, modular construction for shipbuilding was refined to the extent of putting together units complete with all plumbing, wiring and cabin installations.

For decor, Cunard was keen to present a modern look. Traditional wood panelling, parquet flooring and art deco was out. In came expanses of plastics, aluminium, stainless steel and modular green leather furniture on dark carpeting. Abstract art was hung throughout public rooms and cabins.

Inspecting the plans for the public rooms, the Queen Mother pointed at one and asked what it was called. 'It's the Queen's Room, Ma'am.' Her Majesty sniffed and murmured, 'How snobby.'

Equally snobby was the striking, single-scooped, modernistic funnel which, instead of being painted with the usual black and orange, was all black and surrounded by a white scoop. Only the visible inside of the scoop was painted in Cunard orange. It was controversial and in a 1983 refit the funnel reverted to Cunard's traditional horizontal orange and black bands.

With all fitting-out finished, she entered service in 1969. It was a big year for travel: the Concorde supersonic jet was unveiled, and *Apollo 11* blasted off for the first successful manned moon landing. 'One small step for man, one giant leap for Cunard.'

With her sleek, futuristic looks, *QE2* fitted right in as a child of her era. There were some technical teething problems, but slow-to-accept, crusty seafarers were surprised to see how quickly she assumed the majestic mantle of reverence worn by the previous Queens.

History proved her more than entitled to this position. The QE2 earned her stripes by her number of years of service, miles travelled and passengers carried. She even shocked the world by answering her country's call to war and serve as a troop ship. This was, again, another Queen playing a key role in her country's protection.

Cunard had no plans to build an identical running mate to make a regular transatlantic cross-halfway service. Although she had the long-sloped, fine bow needed for the Atlantic in all weathers, in winter she turned to cruising as a one-class ship. This was where abandoning the vertical partitioning of her predecessors and adopting a horizontal division of public areas made a big difference. Although it was not seamless, it did give passengers more of the feeling of having the run of the ship.

Initially, she had the RMS (Royal Mail Ship) prefix. But turning more to cruising and with no running mate, she was forced to abandon this and become SS (Steam Ship) *Queen Elizabeth 2*.

She was the last remaining oil-fired passenger steamship on a scheduled Atlantic service until, in 1986, she rid herself of her trouble-prone steam-turbine engines and gained a new lease of life by installing diesels and a new smoke stack.

These proved more reliable, had the added advantage of reducing fuel needs by 35 per cent and caused QE2 to change her prefix again, this time to MS (Motor Ship).

The lack of a running mate for a transatlantic service led to her sleeping with the enemy. Cunard and BOAC (now British Airways) formed a marketing company, BOAC Cunard, to cross the Atlantic one way by sea and the other by air.

This was ironic as it was BOAC that brought Cunard's own airline ambitions down. In 1960, Cunard had bought a controlling stake in Eagle Airways, hired pilots and a couple of years later signed for two Boeing 707s to fly services to and from New York. However, in a complicated set of backroom deals, BOAC appealed to the British Government, succeeded in having the licence revoked and brought Cunard back to the negotiating table.

That's how it came about that one of my entertainment officer colleagues was in fact an airline pilot, complete with debonair, long and twirly RAF moustache. Employed by Cunard for its proposed airline, he suddenly found there would be no planes to fly and ended up alongside me calling bingo on *Queen Mary*. Yes, we were an odd lot.

The launch of a new Cunard Queen always gets a special greeting. (Paul Curtis)

PERILS AT SEA

QE2 sailed just short of forty years and at that point was the longest serving Queen in Cunard history. She voyaged 5.6 million miles, carried 2.5 million passengers and completed 806 transatlantic crossings. Name me a ship that can top that.

She was often in the news. In 1971, she promptly answered a mayday call from the French cruise ship *Antilles*, which had hit a reef off the Caribbean island of Mustique, ruptured her oil tanks and then burst into flames. Five hundred passengers took to the lifeboats to land on a nearby beach before being tendered to *QE2*. One *Antilles* passenger claimed that the ship swap was worth it.

In 1974, she came to the rescue of six yachtees in the Mediterranean and took them off their sinking sailing yacht.

In 1990, she was called to rescue the forty-nine crew members of a sinking oil rig that had broken loose while being towed in an 80mph storm in the North Sea. With the weather easing, the oil-rig crew forsook the luxury on offer from the world's most famous liner and opted to stay on their imperilled oil rig. It was a poor choice. After *QE2* sailed on, the rig did capsize. Fortunately, no lives were lost.

A year later, when 1,000 miles from New York and on passage to Southampton, the company's New York office received a ransom note saying there were six bombs on board and set to explode unless a demand for $350,000 was met.

With the ship at a stop in mid-ocean and under the watchful eyes of 1,500 disconcerted passengers and crew, a scrambled British Special Air Services bomb-disposal team parachuted into the sea near the ship. They were picked up in lifeboats and brought aboard to help conduct a full search. This was a bit of excitement not found on your average cruise.

However, not a single bomb was found. Did this make the passengers happy? No, now they were even more anxious. Where was that bomb?

There was no big bang: the extortionist had been bluffing. This story ends with the FBI getting their man and his being sentenced to twenty years in jail. That would teach him not to mess with a Queen.

The following year, Muammar Gaddafi hatched a plan to send a submarine to torpedo *QE2* while she was on a Jewish cruise off the coast of Israel. Gaddafi was seeking revenge for Israel's downing of Libyan Flight 114.

Although Cunard had increased security for these waters, passengers were happily partying the cruise away and unaware of the planned attack. Fortunately, Egyptian president Anwar Sadat was not unaware of what Gaddafi was up to as it was one of his submarines Gaddafi was using. He countermanded the order and QE2 was spared. Thus, the ship fared better than Gaddafi as, of course, he was himself later assassinated.

Even in dry dock the ship was not safe from threats. In 1976, the IRA attempted to blow up the ship. No, they didn't burn their lips on the funnel. The three men were arrested and sentenced to twenty years.

The only thing that ever struck the ship was a giant whale. It was 1996 and, off the coast of Portugal, it was more a case of the ship harpooning the poor thing with its bulbous bow. It remained stuck on the ship's nose all the way into Lisbon.

The carcass weighed 15 tons and a crane had to be called in to remove it. A sad case of not having a whale of a time.

IT'S WAR

It is April 1982. The British territories of the Falkland, South Georgia and South Sandwich Islands are amongst the least desirable places in the world to live. Wave-battered and 1,500 miles off the Argentinian coast, they are cold, bleak and lonely. South Georgia and the South Sandwich Islands have not one permanent resident. The only population is on the Falkland Islands, where there are 1,820 proud-to-be-British citizens and 400,000 sheep of unknown nationality preference.

By virtue of proximity, the Argentinians think these islands should be theirs. Why anyone would want them, heaven knows. But to divert attention from its failing home economic policies, the troubled military government invades the islands and takes possession. That should lift morale at home.

Of course, they knew Britain wouldn't like it, but what the heck was she going to do about it? After all, England was 8,000 miles away.

But they had not counted on Britain's first lady Prime Minister, Margaret Thatcher. She was not called the Iron Lady for nothing, and besides, with the strike trouble she was having in Britain, she was quite glad of a little political diversion herself.

Troops exercising on QE2. *(Paul Guest)*

So, act they did. The British immediately put together an invasion fleet of no fewer than 127 ships. This armada consisted of sixty-five naval vessels and sixty-two requisitioned merchant ships. It was a huge task but done in a few weeks and then it was 'look out, here we come'.

However, to us back home, brought up thinking the next war would be all about atomic bombs and nuclear fallout shelters and over in ten minutes, it seems as though time is standing still.

These are the days of duck and cover with community maps directing us to the nearest nuclear fallout shelter. We have maps with coloured rings showing the distance in miles from where the nuke hits to where you are and the exact number of minutes you have before being burnt to a crisp.

Thirty miles and you have twenty minutes to find shelter. Five miles? Don't bother. As our American cousins charmingly say: 'All you can do is bend over and kiss your ass goodbye.'

So, the beginning of the Falklands War is seeming painfully slow. It's taking three weeks to get the ships over there to start the fighting. At Plymouth Hoe, Sir Francis Drake could have played a whole week of bowls, instead of finishing just one game before going off to chuck a match at the invading Spanish Armada.

To the world's surprise, the British Government conscripts as troop ships its two most valuable liners, QE2 and the P&O Canberra. Cruises are cancelled, and passengers are left standing with their luggage on the pier with nowhere to go. The two ships are propelled into a conflict that lasts seventy-four days before Argentina surrenders and returns the islands to British control.

This was no Mickey Mouse war. Seven ships were sunk, nearly 200 aircraft destroyed, thousands wounded, and more than 900 lives lost: 649 Argentine military, 255 British military, and three Falkland Islanders. It was hardly the safest place for Britain to send her most valued liner.

However, as QE2 can travel fast and carry more than 3,000 troops, it was demanded that she serve her country, forcing her to follow in the wake of her Queen Mary and Queen Elizabeth forebears.

In just nine days at Southampton, she is prepared for war. The top decks of the stern are sliced off, pools decked over, and the forward quarterdeck extended over the capstans to create helicopter landing pads. Fuel pipes are fitted for refuelling at sea.

Steel plate is used to reinforce the ship for a quarter of her length and an anti-magnetic coil is added to protect against the menace of naval mines. Thoughtfully, extra lifejackets are also put on.

The ship's 12 miles of luxury carpeting are covered with 2,000 sheets of hardboard. Valuable soft furnishings, paintings and five grand pianos are deemed 'not for the use of troops' and taken ashore for safe storage. Finally, the public lounges are converted into dormitories and now the formerly luxurious QE2 is a warship.

However, in a rare weak moment of kindness, the Admiralty and Cunard decide to leave on board some cases of caviar. But there are no comfortable, Lacoste-wearing, happily rotund passengers in the lounges: just a sea of lean and battle-hardened troops in camouflage fatigues.

With Argentinian submarines and aircraft out looking for her, the blacked out and camouflage-painted QE2 zigzagged for eighteen days on her way to South Georgia Island.

On the voyage, the troops continually exercised around the decks, but the mood remained light. However, this darkened when the equator was crossed, and the news came that the fleet's *Atlantic Conveyor* had been sunk by two Argentinian Exocet missiles. This was no Caribbean cruise. This was war.

Even with the ship's steel-plate reinforcing, there were still large areas of aluminium in QE2's superstructure. She was built this way to save weight, reduce the draught of the ship and lower fuel consumption. But aluminium has a low melting point and if the ship is struck by a missile, as was her co-fleet ship, HMS *Sheffield*, the resulting fire could cause her upper decks to quickly collapse.

This had not seemed to deter the Admiralty's desire to conscript her, but the 650 crew who volunteered to stay and look after the 13,200 members of the 5th Infantry Brigade were a little less sanguine.

On 27 May, QE2 arrived in Cumberland Bay, South Georgia, and the 5th Infantry Brigade was transferred first to P&O's *Canberra* and from there onto the islands.

With the troops delivered, QE2's job is nearly done. On her return trip she becomes a hospital ship and carries home more that 600 of the wounded. Arriving back in Southampton in June, it takes nine weeks and several million pounds to restore QE2 to her former glory before she is able to resume her weekly five-day transatlantic crossings.

So, again she became another Queen that escaped the conflict unharmed.

The only real damage ever encountered by QE2 was self-inflicted. In 1975 the bulbous bow was holed when she struck an incorrectly charted reef at Nassau. Then, in 1992, she ran aground near Massachusetts' Martha's Vineyard. A combination of an uncharted shoal and underestimating the increase in the ship's draught due to the squat effect had her scraping the rocks and having to go for repairs. This squat effect happens when a ship is travelling fast over shallows and is consequently drawn lower into the water.

But the most embarrassing grounding was on her final arrival into her home port of Southampton before being transferred to her new owners in Dubai. In 2008, with 1,700 passengers, 1,000 crew, and with news helicopters and media boats out in force to capture this milestone event, she ran aground right at the river entrance. Five tugs were sent out to pull her off the Brambles sandbank.

She was refloated and then slunk into her home berth where divers were sent down to look for any damage. Fortunately, there wasn't any.

So okay, she touched the seabed three or four times. Over more than 5 million miles and nearly forty years, that's not bad. Many weekend sailors top that every summer.

FACING THE SEAS

No ship goes through thirty-nine years of world cruising and Atlantic crossings without encountering the odd spot of bother with the weather.

In 1976, a very rough sea caused a 12.5 ton anchor to break loose and punch a hole in her bulbous bow. She began to take in water but, with the pumps working flat out, she made it into Boston for repairs.

She was caught in a big Atlantic hurricane in 1978 but the real horror came in 1995, when she had to heave to in the face of 120kt winds from Hurricane Louis, 200 miles off the coast of Newfoundland.

The seas were running at 40 to 50ft when up came a rogue wave estimated at 90ft, or for the metric enabled, 27m high.

According to Captain Warwick, the seething mass of water was like looking at the White Cliffs of Dover. The weight of the water crashing onto the foredeck dented deck plating and bent some of the rails. But all was calm on board.

On another occasion, with QE2 hove to for nearly twenty-four hours in 100mph winds, Captain Arnott wished to give an impression of calm to his passengers by joining them for dinner in the dining room.

Just as he entered, the ship gave a terrific lurch and diners, chairs and crockery went everywhere. The captain braced himself. His instinct was to run to the bridge to check what was happening, but instead, when the ship settled, he proceeded calmly to his table. He was imagining the panic in the dining room if he had turned and fled back to the bridge.

Captain Arnott was also in command when QE2 hit heavy weather in the South China Sea. Undeterred, Welsh comedian Harry Secombe went ahead with his performance for passengers in the Queen's Room.

The Bay of Biscay in frivolous mood as seen through the tinted windows of QM2's *Britannia Restaurant on her maiden voyage. (Paul Curtis)*

After his show, the famous *Goon Show* entertainer sidled up to the captain and said, 'Nice little theatre you have here. Reminded me of a seasick Swansea Empire. It wasn't only my singing that sent the audience for the doors you know.'

Arnott admitted the South China Sea was being a bit rough. 'What!' exclaimed Secombe. 'My agent said we were going to Cardigan Bay!'

Arnott enjoyed the exchange and had already proved himself a captain with a sense of humour when, in command of *Cunard Adventurer*, his bow was slightly dinged in a port-manoeuvre collision. Spotting his sister ship *QE2*, he signalled her 'You may be the Queen of the seas, but we're a little bent too!'

KEEPING UP APPEARANCES

With a career stretching over thirty-nine years, a lady must be kept in the best possible condition and this needs occasional visits to the beauty parlour.

So it was with *QE2*. She had several hull repaints, interior refits and alterations. In 1994, she was given a completely new look with a major refit in Hamburg. Almost all the remaining original decor was replaced and, echoing her predecessor, some art deco managed to find its way back on board.

Four years later, she went for her biggest update: a $30 million make-over resulting from a major cash injection from the American-based Carnival Corporation taking over Cunard. During this refit the hull was stripped to bare metal, and the ship repainted in the traditional Cunard colours of matte black with a white superstructure. Once more, *QE2* could look in the mirror and claim to be the 'fairest of them all'.

In 2004, the transatlantic run was assigned to Cunard's new flagship, *Queen Mary 2,* and *QE2* switched to full-time cruising.

FAREWELL *QE2*

Faced with the expense of meeting some of Britain's strict new legal port restrictions, in November 2008, Cunard retired *QE2*. A Dubai company trumped up $100 million for the deal, but Cunard had inserted one clause that left her future without a conclusion.

Dubai's original plan was to keep her in seaworthy condition and use her as a 500-room hotel ship and tourist attraction at the luxury Palm Jumeirah complex.

The only alteration to the ship before leaving for Dubai was the careful removal of the synagogue. Dubai didn't seem to think they would have a use for that. In fact, in her entire career, the synagogue was the only room on the ship never altered.

She arrived in Dubai from Southampton to the cheers of onlookers, fireworks, a welcoming crowd of thousands and an Emirates jet fly-past. But the party was short-lived as at the same time, the world financial markets collapsed.

The Dubai company found itself in the unenviable position of not having the money to complete the conversion and not being able to sell her. Cunard had inserted a clause in the sales contract that stipulated there could be no onward sale for ten years without payment of another $100 million. As with the previous Queens, this was to protect itself from ever having to compete on the cruise market with its own former ship.

It seems that nobody learned anything from the original *Queen Mary* hotel problems as potential hotel sites were mooted thick and fast. They included South Africa, London, Liverpool, Singapore, Clydebank, Japan and Fremantle, but they all came to nothing. London came closest to securing a deal, but they couldn't work out a way to get a ship of her size through the massive Thames Barrier built for flood protection.

Next came the final ignominy: a rumour that the ship was to be sold to China for $28 million and made into scrap. Fortunately, that idea was also nixed and so she remained empty, rotting and rusting in Dubai. However, in 2018 when the ten years on-sale clause expired, it was announced that she would proceed with the hotel conversion and was fully operational as a hotel by late 2018.

Even without the new lease of life, she has the honour of having consumed the most tons of caviar in a single venue, serving the longest period of any Cunard ship, carrying 3 million passengers and, by courtesy of using the Arabic numeral 2, having the most frequently misspelled ship name in the world.

8 NEVER SAY NEVER: QM2 IS BORN

IN DARKNESS, MY WIFE AND I are standing high on the uppermost deck. Towering above is the ship's floodlit sweeping funnel, a spectacular sight, more Henry Moore sculpture than utilitarian smoke stack. There's a whoomph, a swish and a loud bang as the night sky unexpectedly bursts into showers of bright, sparkling colours. This is just the beginning of a pyrotechnic display of epic proportions.

A continual barrage of fireworks flare into the night sky, flooding the huge ship with a myriad of disco hues. It's a nightclub on steroids. The deafening roar of the ship's whistles joins the cacophony of explosions and the rousing rendition of 'Rule Britannia' blasting from the ship's speakers.

Looking up, I recognise one of the 0.75-ton 7ft steam whistles. I should do. I had sailed under it thirty-seven years before when it was on the original *Queen Mary*'s middle stack. Its resounding boom carries for 10 miles. It has been shipped over from Long Beach on *QE2* to sail the seas once more. For we are now on *Queen Mary 2* departing on her maiden voyage from Southampton in 2004. Never, in maritime history, has a ship received a send-off such as this.

Despite the predictions that the 1960s had seen the end of the great ocean liners, here we are on the largest, longest, tallest, widest and most expensive liner ever built.

This is the first Atlantic liner to be built since *QE2* entered service in 1969 and sixty-six years after the last biggest Cunarder, *Queen Elizabeth*. How could such a ship come into being? Well, we are now ten days into our run and the man who knows the story better than anyone is standing beside me at the rail as we watch dawn break over the Caribbean island of St Thomas.

He is the designer and project manager of *QM2* and we are watching a large cruise ship, *Venture of the Seas*, from rival cruise company Royal Caribbean, anchoring beside us in the bay off Charlotte Amalie. He is telling me that until we arrived, she was the largest ship in the world, but this company is already planning to build a ship bigger than the one we are on. As we are still on our maiden voyage, I express some horror and sympathy that *QM2* is to have such a short reign as the largest. He shrugs, then grins and says, 'But their new ship won't be a liner. This is a real ship!'

And there's the big difference. A liner is a real ship, capable of keeping a schedule across the rough winter seas of the North Atlantic. To breast the huge waves requires a high, long, narrow, sheer and reinforced bow that takes up nearly one-third of the ship. This design does away with many of the high-revenue balcony cabins from the forward part of the vessel. For longevity and strength, steel, not aluminium, must be used. Compounding matters, the heavy weight of steel does away with the ability to build a complete deck of cabins. All this adds about 40 per cent to the costs. This is definitely an expense arena few cruise companies wish to enter.

But this quiet man beside me has managed to talk his hard-bitten employers into this high-risk, $780 million venture. He is a man of modest demeanour, but with a true fairy story so incredible it would even challenge the imagination of Hans Christian Andersen. For this is Stephen Payne, the driving force behind the creation of this amazing new ship.

Born in 1960, Stephen Payne's obsession with ships began at age 5 when he was watching the BBC children's television show *Blue Peter*. They were showing a film of *Queen Elizabeth* and young Stephen was fascinated. Four years later, he persuaded his family to take him to Southampton docks, where he could see the liner for himself.

At age 12, Stephen is still watching *Blue Peter* and the programme is now showing film of *Queen Elizabeth* on fire in Hong Kong. The voiceover is saying nothing like her will ever be built again. Young Stephen is horrified and sends off a protest letter to say they are wrong and another ship to rival her would indeed be built and he was the person who was going to design her and here were his plans and suggestions to prove it.

The programme sent their special *Blue Peter* badge and, while congratulating him on his ambition, cautioned him not to be discouraged if it never happened. But happen it did. And yes, it was Stephen who designed her.

The badge arrived but it was just the standard one. Young Stephen was disappointed. He thought his efforts had warranted the gold badge. Miffed but undeterred, he went on to finish school and enrol in the University of Southampton's Ship Science programme. He followed this with studies at the University Royal Naval Unit on how ships respond at sea.

After graduating in 1984 with a BSc (Hons) in ship science, he commenced a successful ship-designing career. This resulted in him landing a job at Carnival, one of the world's biggest operators of cruise lines, and now the owners of Cunard.

The boss of Carnival, Mickey Arison, had seen the movie *Titanic* and noted the huge wave of nostalgia it developed for the days of the great ocean liners. Thus inspired, Carnival liked the idea of introducing to the

Passengers crowd the decks as a massive firework display launches Queen Mary 2 *on her maiden voyage from Southampton docks. (Paul Curtis)*

world another great ocean liner. And amongst their design team, Arison had just the man for the job: Stephen Payne.

Stephen was passionate in his design approach. Having a thorough appreciation of the history of the early liners, he set out to create a ship with all the majesty of the past, but with the ability to meet modern cruising needs.

Due to the ever-mounting costs, however, on three occasions the Carnival board stopped the project. But Stephen would go back to the drawing board and design another work around.

This included designing a ship that could be turned around on port arrival in one day, rather than the two or three days enjoyed by the previous Queens. Recognising this was going to put more strain on the crews, Stephen designed improved crew facilities and ensured that rather than ten, the maximum occupancy of a crew cabin was two. What a hero!

GET IT RIGHT

He had the special nostalgic support of Carnival CEO Micky Arison because it was the Cunard *Mauretania* that brought his father from Europe to start a new life in the States. Although Arison was entranced with the great ocean liner concept, he warned Stephen, 'I suspect you will only get one chance in your lifetime to design a ship such as this, so you had better get it right the first time.'

Stephen's main design constraints were cost per passenger cabin, the size of the turning basin at Southampton and the height of the Verrazano-Narrows Bridge in New York. His final design just scraped past all three.

He would dearly have liked the funnel to have been higher and that is why he had to design a wind-scoop at the base to give the height of the exhaust some extra boost. He maintains the bridge was built too low and wistfully thinks if a ship-yard was to build a ship too high, the bridge would only be a problem for the first visit.

Stephen did get it right and he did build his dream. Starting in 1998, his final design won through and a contract to build was signed. *QM2* was delivered to Cunard in December 2003, on time and under budget.

QM2 designer Stephen Payne on QM2's maiden voyage. (Paul Curtis)

On the day before the naming ceremony, the *Blue Peter* television programme sent a camera crew to film this extraordinary story. After being given a tour of the ship by Stephen, the programme relented and gave him his gold badge.

John Brown's Glasgow shipyard had built all the previous Cunard Queens, but this time was not in a financial position to bid for the new project and thus its shared 100-year history with Cunard was at an end. Faced with no government support, another British shipyard, Harland and Woolf, withdrew from the running.

Nevertheless, the British were shocked to see Cunard sign the build contract with an old arch-enemy, the French Alstom Chantiers de l'Atlantique shipyard in St Nazaire. It was Chantiers that built famous Cunard competitors, such as the *Normandie* and the *France*. Many thought this was taking Britain's entry into the Common Market a bit too far.

However, the French Government was prepared to back its shipbuilders, while the British Government, tired of over-militant unionism, was not. Nevertheless, many of the former skilled shipyard workers from Scotland and other parts of England went to France to work on the new ship.

Construction began in 2002. The task was enormous. Ever had the heartache of building a house? Try building a ship. There are more obstacles than the Aintree steeplechase.

The ship is 345m long. That's 7m longer than the original *Queen Mary* and therefore equivalent to the length of fifteen blue whales, or four football fields. Or, if you are a Londoner and have endured many a wait for a bus, imagine a long line of thirty-six of them coming along all at once. Don't they always?

The build is about as tall as the Empire State Building, that is if you knock off the spire bit on the top. It took 300,000 pieces of steel, cut and welded into ninety-four blocks. Some of these weighed more than 600 tons. Assembling it together required 1,500km of welding.

Seventeen decks were built, equal to the height of a twenty-three-storey building towering 72m above the waterline. At 41m wide, she cannot squeeze through the Panama Canal. To get to Australia, she must round one of the two southernmost capes.

It took 2,500km of wiring to connect 80,000 lighting points. The lick of paint required 250 tons of paint. The power plant installed is equal to the power of 1,600 cars and could light a city of 200,000 people. Her speed of

30kt is twice the speed of the average Caribbean cruise ship and, maybe more importantly, nearly three times the speed of those blue whales.

If ever QM2 comes across a school of 330 blue whales, as far as weight goes, they will be evenly matched. To avoid them, at her top speed of nearly 30kt, a full emergency crash stop takes three minutes. It's not a decision taken lightly: the test on sea trial produced awesome vibrations and even the bridge shuddered.

Powering the ship along are four pods that hang beneath the waterline like outboard motors. Each one weighs more than a fully loaded jumbo jet. And yet this monster floats.

Altogether, to finish the job it took 8 million man-hours. The total build cost reached $780 million. It was completed on time. This was to be expected after Cunard CEO Pam Conover, at the first steel-cutting ceremony, presented the shipyard chairman with tickets booking him and his wife on the maiden voyage. Said Ms Conover, 'This is one sure way to guarantee that the ship is completed on time.'

There are no rock-climbing walls, dodgem cars or ice rinks on QM2. This is a Cunarder: that means she is a very classy ship. Of all things, there is a massive planetarium on board. You don't even need to go up on deck to look at the stars.

The planetarium is very informative and joins an educational centre with seven classrooms. The ship's library is the largest at sea and has more than 10,000 books, when you include audio and CDs. For art lovers, there are nearly $5 million of commissioned artworks on display. She also has the largest dance floor on a liner and now she is complete and ready to trip the light fantastic on the high seas.

A CRUEL BLOW

However, tragedy strikes. During the final stages of fitting-out there were 2,600 workers boarding and leaving daily across gangways. Just before leaving for sea trials, the yard management decided to treat their workers by letting them bring family and friends for a visit. This meant they would have to handle a lot more people.

To facilitate this, it was decided to install a new gangway just under half a metre wider than the one previously being used. The next day, tragedy struck. With forty-eight people on it, 20m above the concrete floor of the dry dock, it suddenly collapsed. Fifteen people were killed and thirty-two were injured.

Out of respect, work was halted, and her sea trials were delayed. However, when held, they were successful and, with QE2, Cunard now had the two fastest ocean liners in the world.

NAMING CEREMONY

It had been decided to award the ship the honorary prefix of RMS, for Royal Mail Ship. Apart from three other ships which are basically ferries, she is the last great ship to hold this naming prefix.

The ship was delivered to Southampton at the beginning of January 2004 and again Queen Elizabeth turned up to do the naming honours. Standing on the launch platform, the biggest liner ever built towered above her, dwarfing her diminutive form.

She proclaimed, 'I name this ship *Queen Mary 2*. May God bless her and all who sail aboard her' and pushed a button to send a French bottle of Veuve Clicquot smashing against the French-built hull. For the launch of the first *Queen Mary*, a good old bottle of sparkling Aussie Empire wine was used.

At this time, Britain was all Common Market and had turned her regal back on all that Aussie Commonwealth stuff. Never mind that the Aussies and other Commonwealth nations had sent the pride of their young manhood to fight and die for good old Blighty. This was business, and for England that meant pull up the ladder Jack, we're all right with Fortress Europe.

Sorry, was I having a bit of a rave there? Well, Britain has come and gone from Europe, but the Commonwealth remains. How else could we fill our cricket calendars?

Meanwhile, back at the launch, with crowds of spectators and a television audience of millions, QM2 sounds three horn blasts while confetti rains on the crowd, fireworks burst in the sky, flares sprout from the bow and the crowd gives three cheers as *Queen Mary 2* assumes her role as the world's greatest liner.

The televised naming ceremony. (Cunard)

MAIDEN VOYAGE

So here we are, four days later, off on the maiden voyage. We have a full complement of passengers: 45 per cent from the UK, 43 per cent from the States and the rest from all over.

In command is Commodore Ronald Warwick, son of former *QE2* Commodore Bill (Bil) Warwick who commanded *QE2*'s maiden voyage thirty-five years before. Yes, that's right, there is only one 'l' in Bil. He was even more economical with his crew. On *QE2* he had 1,000 crew members. Son Ronald has a crew of 250 more – the largest crew ever assembled for a passenger ship.

The fourteen-day cruise taking her to Fort Lauderdale is first calling at Madeira, Tenerife, Las Palmas, Barbados and St Thomas.

At lifeboat drill, my wife and I discover that, if things go wrong, we will be sharing a lifeboat with Welsh songstress Dame Shirley Bassey. This is along with a disconcertingly large crowd of others.

Dressed in warm clothes, sporting a bulky Mae West lifejacket and behind dark glasses, Ms Bassey is looking less than her usual glamorous self. Still, we guess, she doesn't don a glittering sequined dress when popping out for a bottle of milk. Ah well, we console ourselves, if the ship goes down, in our lifeboat we can at least go out with a song.

At sea and in the Bay of Biscay, we hit 6m waves and a full gale with gusts reaching 70mph. Not the best start, but the ship is surprisingly stable. One bonus is that at lunchtime the massive two-decked Britannia Restaurant is virtually empty. Which is just as well, as many of the new waiters have also been knocked off their feet.

Ms Bassey is unwell and postpones her opening concert. Her place is taken, oddly enough, by a concert pianist aptly and nautically named Marina, who is now married to Captain Aseem Hashmi. Aseem says Marina's trio was not allowed to be seasick. There were few in the theatre, but right there, on the opening days of her first voyage, *Queen Mary 2* proves she is a well-built ship and can take anything the seas can throw at her.

Each arrival of *Queen Mary 2* in the European ports was met with spectacular displays from fire boats shooting colour spumes of water high into the air and huge welcoming crowds at the docks. With news helicopters hovering overhead, the ports maintained full carnival mode all day before sending her off in the evening with another spectacular firework display. It was the stateliest and most celebrated reception any ship has ever received.

KEEPING SAFE

The best was saved till last as she received a spectacular greeting on arrival at Fort Lauderdale with live television coverage on all major networks. Thousands crowded the vantage points at the port entrance. The balconies of the long bordering bank of condominiums were all crammed with waving and cheering people.

Everywhere, security was very tight. US Navy and Coastguard patrol boats with flashing blue lights kept spectator boats at bay, while snipers kept a protective watch from rooftops.

As soon as we docked, an underwater security net was positioned a few yards off from the ship and then patrolled by armed security vessels.

An underwater security net was immediately drawn around the QM2 *as soon as she docked at Fort Lauderdale on her maiden arrival. (Paul Curtis)*

This was to prevent any chance of a frogman attack. Up in the sky, a no-fly zone protected the airspace over the ship.

The al-Qaeda attack on the Twin Towers in 2001 hit the holiday industry hard. Now newspaper reports were saying the terrorist organisation, in its Jihad against the West, was threatening to target luxury liners and specifically mentioned the *QM2*'s maiden voyage.

A US spy plane discovered scores of acoustic sea-mines had disappeared from a naval base in North Korea and US intelligence services feared they could be aboard terror ships assembled by Osama bin Laden. The mines were fitted with homing devices that allowed them to zero in on large targets. And they didn't come any larger than *Queen Mary 2*.

When al-Qaeda's chief of naval operations, Al-Neshari, was captured he was carrying a large dossier listing many big cruise liners in Western ports as 'targets of opportunity'. Fortunately, so far, there have been few incidents involving cruise ships.

Helicopters and fire boats greet QM2*'s maiden arrival at Fort Lauderdale. (Paul Curtis)*

SAILING ON

Apart from her cruise schedule in her first year, QM2 made thirteen transatlantic crossings. This freed QE2 to take up full-time cruising.

As of the beginning of 2018, QM2 had sailed more than 2 million nautical miles, made more than 3,000 Atlantic crossings and carried more than 2 million passengers.

In 2016, she had a major refit to keep her in tip-top condition. Cunard called it a remastering, which sounds a bit like the captain got the chop, but this was definitely not the case.

Altogether, Cunard spent $145 million on the renovations which included fifty new staterooms, new restaurants and ten new kennels for her four-legged travellers. Even some of her artwork was updated. The 5,000-piece collection is worth millions of dollars and includes murals, oil paintings, watercolours, mosaics and bronze and glass sculptures.

Touring the ship in 2017, we found she looked as fresh and exciting as she had on her maiden voyage and ready to give many more years of service.

In the last ten years she had notched up some incredible credentials. She proudly boasted that she was now the largest single consumer of Russian caviar in the history of the entire world: 11,830kg of the stuff. This was washed down with 1.2 million bottles of champagne, and, of course to prove her British credentials, more than 21 million cups of tea.

She even brought her tea and pastries to the aid of a lone Atlantic rower. Mylène Pacquette was making her successful attempt to become the first North American to row solo across the Atlantic. But eighty-three days into her adventure and still with two months to go, she had been hit by a storm and had lost her sea anchors and satellite telephone. After radioing in her predicament, QM2 was requested to rendezvous and deliver her some replacements.

Along with these essentials, Cunard also dropped down a sample high tea which, thanks to its renowned restorative qualities, enabled the French Canadian to complete her voyage.

MAIDEN CELEBRATIONS

A visit by a Cunarder is always a cause for celebration, but for the maiden arrivals of the QM2 in Las Palmas, Madeira, Tenerife and the West Indies it was exceptional. (Paul Curtis)

Greeting QM2. (Paul Curtis)

There is plenty of deck space to enjoy the sun on QM2. (Paul Curtis)

QM2 has many superb sculptural design features. Even the spare propeller blades carried and stored on deck become works of art. (Paul Curtis)

This giant mural on QM2 is a portrait of Cunard-line founder Samuel Cunard and it is made up of thousands and thousands of small photos of the company's ships, as can be seen in the inset. (Paul Curtis)

WELCOME ABOARD
QUEEN MARY 2
Cunard Line flagship

9 RAISING THREE NEW QUEENS

IN 2017 CUNARD IS TRAVELLING WELL and sets out to expand its boutique fleet of ships to total four. Being dealt four Queens in the same hand puts a smile on many a face.

Cunard's renewed confidence in the cruise market began in 2003, five years before *QE2* was to retire. Much had changed in the shipbuilding world and the previous process of architects creating highly individual designs had given way to the process of popping ships out like Model T Fords off Henry's production line.

One of the most successful shipyards is the Italian firm of Fincantieri. Located near the cruise ship haven of Venice, in the last two centuries it has launched more than 7,000 ships — enough to set Helen of Troy spinning in her grave. With 11,000 employees clocking on daily, there is nothing 'domani' about this company.

One of their newer and popular designs with cruise companies is the Vista class. This is 85,000 tons and carries around 1,900 passengers and yet is still able to wriggle through the Panama Canal. And by 'wriggle', I mean wriggle. There are just 12in of clearance each side in some of the locks, as can be seen in the photo (on page 173) of the *Queen Elizabeth*, courtsey of Captain Hashmi. It was to Fincantieri that Cunard now turned for its next ship.

That ship was the *Queen Victoria* and she was such a success that a couple of years later Cunard was back again to order a sister ship for her, the new *Queen Elizabeth*.

Many commentators thought that would be it for many years to come as far as building more Queens was concerned. However, the company was just warming up. In 2017 the company ordered a surprise new ship, this one not to be as big as *QM2* but able to carry more passengers. To be launched in 2022, the new ship will carry 3,000 passengers, nearly 300 more than *QM2*.

True to its history, Cunard is unlikely to release the new ship's name until just before the launch. Much will depend on the monarch on the throne in 2022, but, that aside, the name 'Queen Anne' is running as a popular favourite. This is probably a wild guess based on the fact that *QM2* has suites named Queen Mary, Queen Victoria, Queen Elizabeth and Queen Anne.

Since 1839, it is the 249th ship to serve in the Cunard fleet. If all else fails, Cunard could pick up from the number of Queens it has built and take a leaf out of Apple's book to call her Q7. How about it, Cunard? Just saying.

Before 2017, spotting the difference between Queen Victoria *and sister ship* Queen Elizabeth *used to be easy when you knew to look for the more vertical slope of the* Elizabeth's *aft decks. However, in a $40 million refit in 2017 to the* Victoria, *the top decks were extended to be more like the* Elizabeth's. *This allowed the addition of thirty cabins, a dining room, a new sundeck and a speciality café. Passenger capacity was increased to 2,081. (Paul Curtis)*

QUEEN VICTORIA

In 2003, Fincantieri laid down the first keel for Cunard's *Queen Victoria*. Although work was well underway, a year later Cunard had a corporate rethink and decided to let that one go to another home within the Carnival conglomerate. That ship became known as P&O's *Arcadia*. This freed up Cunard to make some design changes incorporating some of the successful features of *QM2*. So, Cunard had Fincantieri start again.

This time the Vista design was modified to be 11m longer, 5,000 tons larger, and with an extra deck added to increase the passenger capacity to 2,000.

As Cunard makes more direct transatlantic crossings than any other company, the bow is also especially strengthened with increased steel plating. So, although it is the same basic Vista-class hull design, everything is radically different. There are the double-height public rooms, the double-height library, the magnificent restaurant and the Queens Room dance floor: all combined to make for the complete traditional Cunard experience.

Technically, it doesn't make her a liner, but the new design has more of an ocean liner feel. With the black hull topped off with a white superstructure and the soaring scooped red and black funnel you know, unmistakably, you are looking at a Cunarder.

Queen Victoria's public rooms are mostly on the lower level with a corridor on the port side, but without the central corridor of *Queen Mary 2*. However, there is a similar grand lobby with an art-decorated central staircase running through three decks.

As with *QM2*, the library is a major feature when compared to the poor offerings of other ships. *Queen Victoria*'s theatre was the first one to have private boxes. It has all the elegance of the West End's London Palladium.

The build cost racked up to £265 million, she was the second longest ship Cunarder had ever built and she was delivered in December 2007.

She arrived in Southampton to great fanfare and media attention. On the same day, she continued the tradition of Cunard Queens being named by royalty. This time the ceremony was performed by Prince Charles's wife, Camilla, Duchess of Cornwall. Queen Elizabeth was not there.

Although the bottle of champagne hit the bow, it did not break. A second bottle was immediately launched and successfully shattered glass and champagne over the bow. For sailors, however, a second go is not a good omen. Being more Aussie than English these days, I say it goes to prove Cunard should have stuck with the Australian bubbly. It really is good stuff!

For the maiden voyage, Captain Paul Wright was selected. This was a captain who, when asked by his school councillor what he liked doing, said, 'I like looking out the window.' The councillor sniffed and said, 'You will never get a job doing that.' But from the bridge of Cunard's newest liner, daily, he does just that.

Queen Victoria undertook her maiden voyage, a ten-day cruise to northern Europe, before setting out on her first world cruise. She circumnavigated the globe in 107 days. Phileas Fogg would not have been impressed, but it was much better than travelling in a hot-air balloon.

Coincidentally, centuries before her, the first ship to ever complete a world circumnavigation was also called *Victoria*. That voyage took 1,153 days and lasted between 1519 and 1522. Phileas Fogg would have been even less impressed.

On a lesser navigational note, in May 2008 *Queen Victoria* struck a pier in Malta. The ship was still able to keep operating and the incident only happened because the thrusters malfunctioned.

On one trip, far from land, a large bird on the point of exhaustion collapsed on *Victoria*'s uppermost deck. It was cared for by the crew who invited passengers to name her. The winning name was 'Albert'. This was almost as clever as the passengers on *QE2* who, when invited to name an exhausted pigeon that sought respite on her deck, came up with 'Cooee Two'.

We know that women can make better drivers and two years after that, Cunard announced its first female captain, Danish-born Inger Klein Olsen.

The appointment of a female captain was long overdue. She was 43 at the time and it is traditional for the captain of a ship to be referred to by the crew as the 'Old Man'. Inger was neither old, nor, I am reliably informed, a man. But calling her 'The Old Woman' would surely run the risk of being ordered to walk the plank.

THE NEW *QUEEN ELIZABETH*

Chuffed with the cruising success of *Queen Victoria*, in 2007 Cunard went back to the Italian shipbuilding yard with chequebook in hand. For a royal flush they wanted a twin sister with the same heavier bow plating to cope with the transatlantic run, along with a few other modifications.

Of course, she had to be a little bit longer, so they made sure to add an extra 6in. This brought her to 965ft. Also, by making one slight design change, Cunard also increased the gross tonnage by 852 tons to total 90,901 tons.

This was achieved by making the slope of the stern decks more vertical. It might not look quite so pretty from the outside, but it is much better looking on the inside. Apart from making for extra deck space with a covered games deck, all set up for croquet, old chap, it also allows a few more cabins. Thus, *Queen Elizabeth* can carry forty-four more passengers than *Queen Victoria*'s 2,014.

Queen Elizabeth was completed and handed over to Cunard in 2010. Who else should perform the ceremony other than Queen Elizabeth herself?

The ceremony was held in Southampton in October and with such a veteran as the Queen in charge and with four Cunard namings under her royal belt, the ceremony went off in brilliant sunshine without a hitch. The next day the ship set sail on her maiden voyage, taking her to the Canary Islands.

Ship lovers breathed a sigh of relief. Now the revered ship name of *Queen Elizabeth* would no longer be remembered for the crumpled remains of her predecessor rusting on the bottom of Hong Kong's harbour. Instead we had a very modern *Queen Elizabeth* forging her way into a new chapter of maritime history.

One of her saddest moments was in 2013 when British knighted broadcaster David Frost was on board and had a heart attack and died. He was a regular presenter of passenger talks on Cunard and it seems sadly ironic that Sir David, who in the 1980s used to run two talk shows each week on both sides of the Atlantic by frenetically jetting back and forth on Concorde, should finally have a heart attack while leisurely travelling at sea.

THE QUEENS DOWN-UNDER

It takes me seven years to catch up with the new *Elizabeth*. There are not many things that will make me get up at three in the morning, but the chance to see *QM2* and the *Elizabeth* coming into Sydney together is one of them.

However, as I wait in pouring rain and total darkness to board the small ferry Cunard has hired for a few of us diehard fearless media folk, I am having second thoughts about the wisdom of this.

The plan is for us to venture out to the harbour heads to record this momentous occasion for posterity. *Queen Elizabeth* is to enter first, take up a position at a mooring buoy in view of the Opera House and then, with dawn breaking, for *Queen Mary 2* to enter, pass *Queen Elizabeth* and berth across from the Opera House at Circular Quay.

What a photo opportunity this is going to be. A tour de force for Cunard's public-relations people. The beautiful Sydney harbour with the bridge and famous Opera House in the background and the brilliant

Aussie sun shining from low on the horizon. Flash, bang, wallop, wow what a picture, what a photograph.

But now it seems everything is going horribly wrong. This is none of the PR people's fault, poor darlings. It is down to the weather gods, an indecisive harbour authority and seven decades of inept Sydney government.

Braving the rain, waves and gale-force winds, we hang off the Sydney harbour heads waiting and waiting in the darkness for the ships to appear. We are tossing and spinning on the waves like a steel ball bouncing up and down on a roulette wheel.

There is no horizon, everything is black. I am not worrying about losing my breakfast, I haven't had any. And I certainly don't need the coffee and sticky bun the hospitable PR people keep offering.

Time is passing, and no ships appear. The weather is so awful, dawn can't open her eyes and has decided not to bother getting out of bed on such a horrible day. Eventually, a faint glimmer of ship lights appears in the gloom, but this, my Marine Traffic Finder phone app tells me, is not *Queen Elizabeth* but *QM2*. What happened?

The dawn arrival of two Queens in Sydney Harbour was meant to be a special photo opportunity. However, here we see **QM2** *arriving in pouring rain and total darkness. (Paul Curtis)*

It turns out that the port authority has decided that the harbour mooring buoy facility for the *Elizabeth* is not secure enough to prevent her from swinging across the channel in the strong wind and thus block the *QM2*'s passage to dock at the quay. And the authorities have ruled that *QM2* must be securely berthed before the *Elizabeth* can even enter the harbour. Bang goes that royal rendezvous photo opportunity.

It is pathetic that a city as big as Sydney cannot berth two large ships at the same time. This is because the city's fathers have done nothing to improve the docking facilities for large ships since in the 1940s when the original *Queen Mary* and *Queen Elizabeth* couldn't get into the harbour at the same time.

In spite of the poor harbour facilities, Australians have taken the Queens to their hearts and always give the ships rapturous greetings when they come to Sydney. This loyalty possibly stretches all the way back to when the original Queens first met off Sydney, and thousands of Australian troops, airmen and nurses were given free trips. You didn't have to pay when you were being carried off to war.

After our abortive boat ride, our media party is taken onto *QM2*, so we can see for ourselves the results of the $114 million makeover in 2016. She certainly looks sparkling: brand new and just out of the box. Fifty new staterooms have been added, fifteen of which are for single travellers. The company also added ten new kennels. These are for dogs.

Cunard Australia Chairman, Ann Sherry, proudly points out that Australia is the company's third-largest market and the company is all set for rapid expansion. Onto the winners' podium in first place for largest market is Great Britain. Second place goes to the USA.

So, with a little parochial bias, I cheekily point out that on a percentage of population basis, Australia is Cunard's largest market. Ann is eager to get more visits to Australia by the Queens and with a new one on the building blocks, these chances are greatly increased.

A day later, in brilliant sunshine, my wife and I are aboard *Queen Elizabeth* on the Sydney to Japan leg of her world cruise. She might have sprung from the same womb as *Victoria* and has many things very similar, but in others she is very different.

It's much the same layout and both ships have displays paying homage to Cunard's maritime history. On *Queen Elizabeth*, showcases pay tribute to the two previous *Queen Elizabeths*. Even the decor evokes the art-deco style of the original *Queen Elizabeth*'s 1930s era. On *Queen Victoria*, in keeping with the ship's namesake, the decor is more art nouveau and, dare I say it, a little less traditionally British.

HOW BRITISH IS CUNARD?

Both ships have the feel of true ocean liners. Standing beneath the romantic lighting of ornate chandeliers, you sniff the luxury of rich wood panelling and gleaming marble floors.

The shopping area is reminiscent of strolling through London's Burlington Arcade. The theatres are ornate and, complete with their grand boxes, make you feel as if you're in the West End. Sitting in the theatre at sea on *Queen Elizabeth* is almost disorientating. It is based on the designs of Frank Matcham, whose theatres include the London Coliseum, the London Palladium and the Victoria Palace.

The general British illusion is intensified by visits to the Golden Lion pubs or the magnificent two-storey libraries. As with her sisters, this new *Elizabeth* does feel very British and it is easy to forget that Cunard is now owned by one of the world's biggest shipping groups, which is based in Miami. However, the American office recognises the importance of keeping the ship British and has been smart enough to leave the running to its Cunard Southampton office.

On board, the officers and staff are mainly British, but the crews, the waiters, deckhands and cabin stewards are around 40 per cent Filipino. Added to this is a mix of around fifty other nationalities.

Some of the crew members are coming from a third generation of Cunard staff. From both a crew and passenger point of view Cunarders are very much international ships, but with a huge helping of roast beef and Yorkshire pudding.

I have to say I think the mixed nationality crews are an improvement on some of the 100 per cent British crews I sailed with in days of yore. Before the militant seamen trade unions self-destructed the sailing life of its own members in the 1960s, stewards were mainly recruited from blunt-speaking Liverpudlians, incomprehensibly accented Clydeside-dwellers and drawling Hampshire hogs.

Good folk that they are, these poor darlings rarely managed to get the whole service concept exactly right. They often approached their service duties with either an air of lordly superiority, or with a hearty and heavy dose of over-familiarity.

Much of their pride came from working on a Queen, and they were thus inclined to feel superior to their colleagues on England's other main shipping company, P&O. There was an endless war of jibes and barbs conducted between the crews of the two shipping companies. Cunarders, we claimed, carried the cream of society to and from Europe and the States, whereas P&O carried migrants and refugees down to Australia and New Zealand. And who would want to go there?

The English crews did have their sense of humour, though. In the 1960s, England had a notorious reputation of requiring a penny to be put into the locking slot of public toilets. When the boat train, packed with overseas visitors with no opportunity to get English coinage, arrived from Southampton at London's Waterloo station, it was not unusual to see people, in their desperation to get to the toilets, jump the coin-operated turnstiles.

Back in the 1960s, on the first night at sea one steward with a keen sense of humour would attach a penny-in-the-slot mechanism to open the cabin's bathroom door. Arriving on board and being confronted with this, some poor American ladies would protest they couldn't be expected to find an English coin every time they wanted to go to the bathroom. Inevitably they would seek a negotiation to settle-up for access at the end of the voyage.

To this the steward would haughtily reply, 'Madam! This is a Cunarder … not a P&O.'

He would then burst into gales of laughter to make sure they got it just as you did, quick as a flash. After removing his dummy mechanism, he would then move on to play the same trick on another cabin. At the end of the voyage, he always scored well in tips for his humour and special bathroom access rights.

So, no, you don't need a British penny to visit the bathroom on a Cunarder. Which is just as well, as on QM2, for instance, there are 2,000 of them. Besides, the on board currency on all Cunard ships is now the mighty United States dollar. Not much British about that.

LICENSED TO MARRY

In 2011, Cunard decided to abandon 171 years of history by transferring the registration of its ships from Britain to the Bermudan port of Hamilton. This meant that on the stern of the ships the name Southampton was welded and plated over with the port name Hamilton. However, the British Merchant Navy Red Ensign is flown without the addition of the Bermudan Coat of Arms on the fly corner.

Cunard said the move was to enable weddings to be solemnised while at seas. A very good reason too, but an awful cynic might point out that the move also saved Cunard from thousands in taxes as well as freeing itself from Britain's self-destructive maritime unions and regulations. That cynic would be me.

Am I right to be a tad sceptical? While sitting in the master's study on *Queen Elizabeth*, I put this question to Captain Aseem Hashmi.

Holding the company line, he proudly shows me his Bermudan-issued certificate authorising him to conduct marriages. He explains that with this certificate he can only perform marriages in international waters.

Many of Cunard's passengers want to marry at sea and it is not company policy to get in the way of true love. However, there will be no Las Vegas roulette weddings. Passengers must give three months' notice. So, go drink all you like at night with no fear of waking up married.

America has a small loophole in which a USA-flagged ship operator allows a properly registered person to perform the ceremony according to the laws of the state in which the ship is docked. But this doesn't have quite the same romantic touch as a ceremony on the high seas. It does, however, have the opportunity of at least getting the marriage off to a less rocky start.

In British law, there is no such loophole. The statute came into being as it used to be that a marriage ceremony must be held in a public space assessible to all. That was for the call, 'If any person here can show cause why these two people should not be joined in holy matrimony, speak now or forever hold your peace.'

A pregnant pause, regardless of the bride's condition, follows. Obviously, on a ship bouncing up and down somewhere in the middle of the Atlantic, a potential objector had less chance of fronting up.

Previously, only one Cunard captain managed to perform a wedding ceremony, but it was under very special circumstances. In 2001, the daughter of *QE2* master Captain Ron Warwick had been due to get married in the port of New York City in a ceremony to be performed by the ship's chaplain, Robert Willing, who despite the back-to-front white collar was a jolly friendly chap, very popular with passengers. He was also Archdeacon Emeritus of New York.

However, when the Twin Towers disaster struck on 11 September, the liner was diverted to Boston, where the Archdeacon was not licensed to perform weddings. The couple particularly wanted to get married on *QE2* as the bride's grandfather had been her original master and the ship had played a large part in their family life.

When Captain Warwick downloaded the rules of matrimony for Massachusetts, he discovered that, with special permission from the Governor of the State, he could perform the ceremony himself. Strings were hastily pulled, and in a fairy-tale ending, permission was granted just in time for *QE2*'s docking. Let's hope they lived happily ever after.

WILL THE NEW QUEENS GO TO WAR?

The talk about marriage now flows into a discussion on war. It's a natural progression. Captain Aseem Hashmi treats my line of questioning with good humour. He is certainly a new broom on a ship's bridge.

Born and bred in Coventry, at the time he first took command, he was the youngest captain ever appointed to a Cunard Queen. He is not your usual style of captain and is far from the bluff and dominating mould I sailed under. He is friendly, has a keen sense of humour and a total dedication to the concept that command is a team project. He has also been awarded the Merchant Navy Medal for his work on crew welfare. Along with the other officers, he mostly does tours of three months on duty and three months off.

The merchant navy was not his first career choice. He was formerly a British Airways trainee pilot and thought his office would be a cockpit. Now, his office is the ship's bridge and although the view is not as high, he most definitely prefers it. Although years ago, I had known Eagle Airlines pilots working on the Queens as pursers and entertainments officers, few airline pilots make it to captain of a major cruise liner.

Although none of the current Queens have been called up for war service so far, all their predecessors have. While the ships were Southampton registered, the British Government could call them up anytime, regardless of the owner. I ask the captain, now the ships are Bermudan registered and American owned, could the British still conscript them for war duty?

It is a complex issue. Bermuda is a British Overseas Territory and as far as the Territories go, you don't get more British than Bermuda. However, it is self-governing and independent of Britain, although only for internal affairs.

Britain has a controlling interest in matters concerning the judiciary, police and, most importantly, defence. So, it appears that in a war situation, Britain could still call on the Queens.

Many Cunard officers are also members of the Royal Naval Reserve and undertake annual training. You will know when you have such a captain aboard as the Blue ensign will be flying from the stern. But let us hope it is only in peacetime. Cunard's Queens have already more than done their share of war duty.

LONG MAY THEY REIGN OVER US

So, what's different about passenger life like aboard a Cunard Queen? Firstly, there is none of the fairground atmosphere of zip lines, carousels, dodgem cars and robot bar tenders. This is Cunard. Sniff. Instead, you will find classes in everything from computer training, seamanship, cooking, art, wine appreciation, languages and photography to, of course, bridge.

Then there is the dancing. Pack your formal gear and get ready to dance the light fantastic in the Queens' large ballrooms. Bellboys will show you the way and gentlemen hosts will make sure no lady goes unpartnered.

Then we come to a Cunard high tea. What is it about tea and the English? It's a sacred ritual performed before the high altar of the teapot. And just as with religion, it comes in a variety of forms. Historically, for the working classes there was no time for shirking around in the afternoon. So, after finishing a hard day's toil at the coal face of industry, 'Tea' was the meal and it was accompanied by a good strong cuppa. The more genteel, however, would take their afternoon tea leisurely in low, comfortable chairs while relaxing in either their parlour or their garden. High society opted for a more formal sitting arrangement of proper chairs and small tables to hold their delectable selection of sandwiches and cakes. The Scottish went one better and included cheese on toast and other savoury goodies.

So high tea and high society go together and for many middle-class people their best opportunity to practice high tea socially was on a Sunday. Being invited to Sunday high tea in the 'front' room by a classy family could prove a social trial sufficient to break sweat from the brows of more humble mortals. It was a time for the very best performance of keeping up appearances. Strict dress code to be observed, no cracking of corny jokes, sit up straight, speak when you are spoken to and hold the cup and saucer in your fiercely scrubbed hands just right, with the little finger angle cocked just so. No, not like that, like this.

For many young men, it was the nerve-racking inquisition time when your girlfriend finally decided it was time for you to meet her parents. This big occasion frightened my brother to death. Eyeing the pepper and salt for his tiny triangular cucumber sandwiches, he distinguished himself by politely requesting in his best voice, 'Please pass the contraceptives.' An arctic silence followed. Eventually, the father leant forward to pick up the condiment set and said, 'Perhaps you mean these?'

English Midlands comedian Jasper Carrott tells the story of when his girlfriend invited him to meet her very posh family and of the disaster that inevitably followed. Things were going very awkwardly, when into the stilted atmosphere of the front room wandered the family labrador. Sitting down in the middle, it bent forward and proceeded to nose around its nether regions. A long awkward silence followed until Jasper felt compelled to say something. Admiring the flexibility of the dog, Jasper said, 'Corr, that's a clever trick. Wish I could do that.'

After a very long pause the lady of the house smiled sweetly and said, 'If you give him a biscuit, perhaps he'll let you.'

On Cunard, as at the Ritz, the daily ritual of serving high tea is still a hallmark of life on the Queens. The current fleet of Queens has already dished up more than 5 million English scones with 320 tons of jam and 312 tons of clotted cream. Imagine that. Not all at once, this is an elegant occasion.

The waiters are white-gloved and carry their salvers of cucumber sandwiches and cakes with hushed footsteps. Rarely, however, do they have the look of the old British family retainer. They are mostly Filipinos in Jeeves clothing. And they move faster.

But Cunarders are still a little floating piece of England. Arrive at a British port and you're likely to hear 'Rule Britannia' and 'Land of Hope and Glory' blasting from the ship's public address system. It is stirring stuff … even for the Welsh.

Building the biggest is not what it takes to make a great ship. After all, they are just huge sheets of cold metal. The reverence and affection that can sometimes develop comes from special ingredients: the people who built her, the people who manage her and the people who sail her. If everyone in the chain adds a touch of tradition, a respect for the sea, dedication, commitment and humour, then you have all the makings of a great ship.

Cunard has managed to do this for more than 150 years. Every one of the line's ships has a great story. When I started my cruising life, many of us were true ship lovers. We knew the name, line and tonnage of every passenger ship afloat. But those were simpler days. We did not have much in the way of leisure diversions.

Our main source of entertainment was the radio programmes, and for transportation we used a bicycle. In those days, even trains had character and we would go train spotting, collecting photographs, and note the class and number of every steam engine. Sadly, some never grew out of it.

Believe it or not, when very young, I used to sit for hours on a drain culvert at the end of our untarred village road and wait, with special notebook in hand, to write down the registration number and make of any previously unseen car that happened to pass by. It might take a week to get a new number. Thousands of other young boys all over Britain were doing the same. And we all lived for the day when the police would politely request to see our notebooks to help them track down some criminal activity. Ah yes, those were the days. Thank heavens they're gone.

Now we have more fun with more intellectual diversions: such as showing pictures on Facebook of what we had for lunch, following idiot celebrities on Twitter and playing Pokémon in strange places.

There are now more than 300 cruise ships, which, although still impressive to look at, means they have lost their novelty. In fact, one cruise-line company became so bored with naming its ships that it gave up and just named them in numerical order, so they went R1, R2, R3 and so on. To treat ships like that, they deserved to go broke. And they did.

Alas, while the number of cruise ships has grown so dramatically, the number of genuine ship enthusiasts has dwindled away. Any author of cruise-ship books can tell you that. But there are still a few diehard fans left, god bless 'em. Where taking a cruise was once the adventure of a lifetime, now it is more like popping out for more milk.

People go on cruises several times a year and when they come back they often can't tell you the name of the ship they were on, or what company she belonged too.

Cunard has managed to defy the shroud of anonymity that now envelops most cruise ships. Every passenger seems to know the brand and the name of each Queen they have cruised on.

Cunard manages to build new ships that not only attract shipping enthusiasts but make new ones as well. How do they breathe life and character into 90,000 tons of twisted metal glued together by a mixed national group of hard-bitten, shipyard welders?

Cunard boasts the proudest past of any shipping company in the world and it is this sense of history that has been imbued into their ships' steel and gives them a heart.

It was Cunard ships that carried to the Crimea the horses that charged with the Light Brigade. Three of the Queens have gone to war for Britain. It was a Cunard ship, the little *Carpathia*, which sped through icefields in the dark to rescue the survivors of the *Titanic*. Every year since 1840, without fail, in peace and in war, Cunard liners have criss-crossed the Atlantic, weaving together the United Kingdom, the United States and Canada.

Transatlantic liners are the thread that runs through Cunard history. It was the first company to offer scheduled transatlantic crossings; and though many others have come and gone, Cunard alone is the only shipping company to continue to do so.

For the last six decades there has always been a Cunard Queen on the seas. With today's fleet of three Queens already cruising the world and a fourth on the building blocks, it is sure that the Cunard tradition will continue for many more decades to come. Long live the Queen.

10 PIECES OF EIGHT

PIECES OF EIGHT, as every good parrot and reader of Robert Louis Stevenson's *Treasure Island* would know, were Spanish silver dollars in circulation between the sixteenth and nineteenth centuries.

Coins were made of precious metals such as silver and gold and the weight of the coin determined its value. Confusingly, a piece of eight was a whole that could be cut into eight pieces to provide different values.

The exchange rate was sixteen full silver pieces of eight for one gold doubloon. You see, once money did have real value. Try getting that at your bank today! If you do, it's best done with a Cornish accent, lots of rolling ahr-ahrrs and a parrot perched on your left shoulder. Crutch sticks optional.

TONS OF FUN

First off, let's understand that gross tonnage is all about the volume inside of a ship and not its actual weight. The biggest cruise ships of today can reach more than 250,000 tons. The actual mass of such a ship, displacement tonnage, is estimated by the weight of the water it displaces. For the biggest cruise ships, this can be about 100,000 metric tons. This is slightly less than that of an American Nimitz-class aircraft carrier.

The difference between 'ton' and 'tonne' is that a 'ton' is a British and American measure, while a 'tonne' is a metric measure. The term derived from an old English term for a barrel of wine called a tun. This refers to the volume of wine tuns that could be carried on board to bring from France to England – a noble calling if ever there was one.

A 'tonne' is equal to 1,000kg. In the US it may be referred to as a metric ton.

The British ton, which is also used in other countries that use the Imperial system of weights and measures, is equal to 2,240lb or 1,016.047kg. It is sometimes referred to as the 'long ton', 'weight ton' or 'gross ton'.

The North American ton, which is only used in the United States and Canada, is equal to 2,000lb or 907.1847kg. It is sometimes referred to as the 'short ton' or 'net ton'.

The difference dates from the nineteenth century when the British adapted the avoirdupois system to create the more easily convertible Imperial system. The Americans continued to use the old avoirdupois units.

This also explains why there are differences between other British and American measures, most notably pints and gallons – and why the English measure their body weight in stone while the Americans use pounds. To an Englishman, their weight in pounds sounds truly worrying and can force them into a premature diet. But these different measures do have specific applications in particular fields of industry, commerce and, of course, shipping.

As we are dealing here with ships, the term gross tonnage, abbreviated as GT, is an index related to a ship's overall internal volume. So, gross tonnage is different from gross register tonnage.

Remember, neither gross tonnage nor gross register tonnage is a measure of the ship's displacement (mass) and should not be confused with terms such as deadweight tonnage or displacement. If you get into a bath naked (recommended) and the bath is filled to the brim, the weight of the water that flows over the side would be your own displacement. Go try it. But don't then run down the street stark naked yelling 'Eureka'. It takes a Greek to do that.

Gross tonnage, along with net tonnage, was adopted by the International Maritime Organization in 1969. These two measurements replaced gross register tonnage (GRT) and net register tonnage (NRT).

Gross tonnage is used to determine things such as a ship's manning regulations, safety rules, registration fees and port dues. The older gross register tonnage was a measure of the volume of only certain enclosed spaces on the ship and did not include engine rooms and crew cabins. So, there you have it. Got it? Phew. Glad we now have that one all cleared up, huh?

WHO WAS THAT?

Aboard ship you will notice a variety of officers' uniform insignias. Worn on the sleeve of a jacket or, in tropical waters, on a shirt as an epaulette, the colour and the number of stripes tells you just who's who in the zoo.

They do vary from line to line, but first check the colour of the space between the stripes. If it is white, it signifies that it is a member of the hotel management. If it is purple, you have just spotted an engineer or electrician. Red is a colour you hope only to meet socially. It signifies medical. Green is used to indicate communications, or what used to be called

On Cunard, from left to right: captain's secretary, marine supervisor, third officer, second officer, security officer, chief officer, deputy captain, captain and commodore.

radio officers. These days it's more about email than knowing Morse code. Watch out if it's bronze: that means the ship's police or security. If there is no colour at all between the stripes, then that means the wearer is a bona fide deck officer, in charge of navigational duties.

Okay, so now we come to the stripes. Obviously, the more the better. Four stripes and you have just met one of the real heavies. It could be the head of the hotel staff, the staff captain or the chief engineer. If the first of the four stripes is double width, you have just met the captain, or sometimes, the most senior man in that department.

Three-stripers are also very senior and indicate a first officer, a doctor or a head purser, depending on the colour in between the gold stripes.

Two and a half stripes indicate a senior second officer, two stripes a second officer and one and a half stripes a third officer. If there is only one thin gold braid going sideways then they are only a cadet. However, they generally have the advantage of being much younger.

The most noticeable change in uniform is when a ship enters the tropics. The officers suddenly ditch their regular navy-blue uniforms and appear in their tropical white rig. These are referred to as 'number tens', dating from when naval uniforms ranged from a reefer jacket to full regalia and were each given numbers. This must be the origin of the term 'dress code'. Mustn't it?

UNTYING KNOTS

The knot (kt) is a unit of speed to cover one nautical mile in one hour. It is nothing to do with knickers. What is a nautical mile? Well, that is 6080.22ft. To convert to land miles per hour, you multiply the speed in knots by 1.15.

Why such an odd distance? Well, we are not on land but at sea. So, one nautical mile is one minute of arc on a circle of the earth. See, it begins to make sense. You didn't expect that, did you? The world is assumed to have a sphere of radius of 3,959 miles, and by measuring in minutes of arc, it makes it easy to find the distances along great circles. Doesn't it?

It might sound like taking the long way around, but because the earth is not flat, it is actually the shorter route system used by ships to travel long distances.

MEASURING UP

The length of a ship can be the length overall (LOA) or the length between perpendiculars (LBP) at the waterline. The depth is measured from the keel to the upper continuous deck. The draught is measured from the keel to the waterline of the loaded ship. The beam is the width of the ship. The front of the ship is the bows; the rear is the stern. The starboard side is the right side when facing the front of the ship and the port side is to the left. Simple, isn't it?

BELLS AND DOGWATCHES

This age-old measurement of a sailing ship's time is still in use today. Originally, a glass timer was used with just enough sand to take half an hour to run into the bulbous chamber. At the end of the half hour, the ship's boy would ring the ship's bell to denote half an hour had just passed and the glass had just been turned over. It also assured the crew that the boy had not fallen asleep.

Starting at midnight, on the first half-hour, the boy would strike one bell and on the second half-hour would strike two bells and so on until at the end of four hours a total of eight bells were tolled. And that meant that the standard four-hour watch for bridge officers was completed. They then needed a break as they probably had a headache from all that bell ringing. The system started over for the next watch. So, if you were in a deep sleep, and you heard two bells, you knew it was 1.00 a.m., or possibly 5.00 a.m. or, if you had been into the rum and really overslept, it could be 1.00 p.m. The light streaming through the porthole gives a clue.

Nowadays, the ship's boy has been allocated a new duty: to wind the brass clock once a week so that never goes to sleep at all. Simple enough so far? Okay. Now we come to the 'dog' watches. To give each man a different watch each day and allow the entire crew to eat an evening meal, the hours between 16:00 and 20:00 are divided into two 'dog' watches with the first dog watchmen eating at 18:00. No canines are involved.

If you ever hear sixteen bells being struck, happy New Year! At midnight it's eight bells for the old year and eight bells for the new.

Accurate time keeping is particularly important for successful navigation and to make sure you never miss the sun going over the yardarm.

TOEING THE LINE

Have you ever looked at the side of a ship and wondered what the little lines marked on the hull are about? Well, there was a time when some shipping companies could be hard, mean and ruthless – imagine that. Nothing like the gentle, kind, fun-loving lot we have today.

Well, back in the bad old days in the freight business, the shipowners liked to load up their ships with as many goods and people as possible.

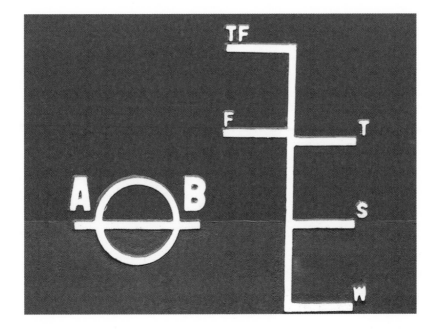

The more the ships could carry, the more the ship owner could carry to the bank.

This could lead to terrible overloading, and out on the open sea, this caused many ships to sink. While passengers and crews lost their lives, these shipowners lost nothing. They had their ships well insured. If the ship was getting old, some owners were so unscrupulous they would deliberately overload them, so they would sink and then just claim the insurance money. Monsters.

In 1875, along came a marvellous gentleman called Sir Samuel Plimsoll, a member of the British House of Commons. He campaigned fearlessly on behalf of sailors and in 1875 introduced into Parliament a bill that stated every ship must have a mark on the waterline showing the limit to which it could be safely loaded.

It was a battle in Parliament to get it through as shipowners were a powerful lobby group. But Plimsoll won, and the bill was passed. To this day, ships around the world are required to show this safe-loading mark. It is called the Plimsoll Line and shows varying draughts according to the salinity of the various seas.

When the soft shoes came along, their design was reminiscent of a Plimsoll Line, and that is how plimsolls got their name.

LINER LINGO

Forward and Bow are the pointy end that comes first. Aft is the back end that comes last

Port is on the left when facing forward.

Starboard is on the right when facing away from aft. Amidships is, you guessed it, the middle of a ship, both laterally and longitudinally.

Companionways are staircases.

Bulkheads are walls.

Bilge is the inside bottom of the ship and sometime dinner talk.

Deck heads are ceilings.

Scuttles is the name used on Cunard for portholes. Leave one open in a rough sea and you could scuttle the ship.

Fiddles, or 'twiddlies' as they are called on Cunard, are the raised edges on tables to stop things sliding off.

Burma Road is the Cunard name for the main internal alleyway used by crew.

Strap-up means clean the silver.

Ahr-ahrrs me hearties means you are a Hollywood pirate.

Yardarm is used for rigging sails or flags. Once the sun is over it, drinks can be served. For this reason, it should be mounted as low as possible.

GOING CONTINENTAL

For this book we have mainly tried to stick with the UK system of measuring and weighing things. However, if you are wanting to convert some facts to metric, try the following guidelines:

I metre ≈ 3.26 feet
I kilometre ≈ 0.62 miles
I litre ≈ 0.26 gallons
I kilogram ≈ 2.20 pounds

ACKNOWLEDGEMENTS

My thanks to the many people who have helped me put this story together. In particular: Stephen Payne, *Queen Mary 2*'s chief architect, Captain Aseem Hashmi, while master of the new *Queen Elizabeth*, Robert Howie, while serving as Hotel General Manager of *Queen Elizabeth*, Paul O'Laughlin while cruise director of *Queen Elizabeth*, John Consiglio, social host on *Queen Elizabeth*, Anne Sherry on the 2017 occasion of the meeting of QM2 and the new *Queen Elizabeth* in Sydney harbour, maritime historian Chris Frame, marine artist Stephen Card and both Jack Frost and his colleague Neil Potter from many years ago while serving on the original *Queen Mary* and we were contributing colleagues to the *Southampton Evening Echo*. Their books on each of the first three Queens are particularly recommended reading. Thanks also to The History Press, in particular Amy Rigg, Martin Latham, and Jezz Palmer. Thanks to Jasper Carrot for allowing me to pinch one of his great anecdotes. I also acknowledge the help of Michael Gallagher and the other members of the Cunard's public relations team in both Britain and Australia.

On the home front I would like to thank my long-suffering family, Peter Edwards, Abi Simpson and Don Richardson for help with the tedious task of proofreading. Great editing advice was provided by Captain Aseem Hashmi and travel writer guru Michael Woolley. Any errors that managed to sneak through are all my own work.

We also acknowledge the archives of:

British Gaumont News
British Pathé News
Daily Express – London
Daily Telegraph – London

FURTHER READING

If we have whetted your appetite for more stories of the Queens, please look out for these books from excellent authors:

Captain of the Queen, Captain Robert Arnott (New English Library, 1982)
Queens Company, Commodore Don MacLean (Hutchinson of London, 1965)
I Captained the Big Ships, Commodore Thelwell (A. Barker, 1961)
The Queen and I, Commodore Geoffrey Marr (Coles, 1973)
Commodore, Commodore James Bisset (Angus & Robertson, 1961)
QE2, Commodore Ronald Warwick (The History Press, 2019)
Tramp to Queen, Captain Treasure-Jones (The History Press, 2008)
The Cunard Story, Chris Frame and Rachelle Cross, (The History Press, 2011)
175 Years of Cunard, Chris Frame and Rachelle Cross (The History Press, 2015)
Evolution of the Transatlantic Liner, Chris Frame and Rachelle Cross (The History Press, 2013)
Queen Mary, Neil Potter and Jack Frost (George G. Harrap & Co., 1971)
Queen Elizabeth, Neil Potter and Jack Frost (George G. Harrap & Co., 1965)
Queen Elizabeth 2, Neil Potter and Jack Frost (George G. Harrap & Co, 1969)

ABOUT THE AUTHOR

Paul has worked as a columnist for the national press, been an editor and publisher of several enthusiast and trade publications and consulted in marketing and communications – all while mostly either working on large ships or small boats. On the art of taking a good snap, he has been a frequent lecturer and commentator for television, radio and the press. Apart from his maritime life, Paul is an Honorary Fellow of the Australian Institute of Photography. This explains why some of his photos are in focus.

Paul likes to hear from his readers and can be contacted at: paul@ paulcurtis.com.au

The destination for history
www.thehistorypress.co.uk